P9-API-076

ELECTRONICS FOR KIDS

ELECTRONICS
FOR KIDS

PLAY WITH SIMPLE CIRCUITS AND EXPERIMENT WITH ELECTRICITY!

BY ØYVIND NYDAL DAHL

no starch
press

San Francisco

ELECTRONICS FOR KIDS. Copyright © 2016 by Øyvind Nydal Dahl.

All rights reserved. No part of this work may be reproduced or transmitted in any form or by any means, electronic or mechanical, including photocopying, recording, or by any information storage or retrieval system, without the prior written permission of the copyright owner and the publisher.

Printed in Canada

First printing

20 19 18 17 16   1 2 3 4 5 6 7 8 9

ISBN-10: 1-59327-725-3
ISBN-13: 978-1-59327-725-3

Publisher: William Pollock
Production Editor: Riley Hoffman
Cover Illustration: Garry Booth
Interior Design: Beth Middleworth
Developmental Editor: Jennifer Griffith-Delgado
Technical Reviewer: John Hewes
Copyeditor: Julianne Jigour
Compositor: Riley Hoffman
Proofreader: Paula L. Fleming

For information on distribution, translations, or bulk sales, please contact No Starch Press, Inc. directly:
No Starch Press, Inc.
245 8th Street, San Francisco, CA 94103
phone: 415.863.9900; info@nostarch.com
www.nostarch.com

Library of Congress Cataloging-in-Publication Data

Names: Nydal Dahl, Øyvind, author.
Title: Electronics for kids : play with simple circuits and experiment with
    electricity! / by Øyvind Nydal Dahl.
Description: San Francisco : No Starch Press, [2016] | Audience: Ages 10+ |
    Includes index.
Identifiers: LCCN 2015048986 (print) | LCCN 2016005706 (ebook) | ISBN
    9781593277253 (pbk.) | ISBN 1593277253 (pbk.) | ISBN 9781593277475 (epub)
    | ISBN 1593277474 (epub) | ISBN 9781593277482 (mobi) | ISBN 1593277482
    (mobi)
Subjects: LCSH: Electronics--Juvenile literature. | Electronic
    circuits--Juvenile literature.
Classification: LCC TK7820 .N93 2016 (print) | LCC TK7820 (ebook) | DDC
    621.381--dc23
LC record available at http://lccn.loc.gov/2015048986

No Starch Press and the No Starch Press logo are registered trademarks of No Starch Press, Inc. Other product and company names mentioned herein may be the trademarks of their respective owners. Rather than use a trademark symbol with every occurrence of a trademarked name, we are using the names only in an editorial fashion and to the benefit of the trademark owner, with no intention of infringement of the trademark.

The information in this book is distributed on an "As Is" basis, without warranty. While every precaution has been taken in the preparation of this work, neither the author nor No Starch Press, Inc. shall have any liability to any person or entity with respect to any loss or damage caused or alleged to be caused directly or indirectly by the information contained in it.

ABOUT THE AUTHOR

Øyvind Nydal Dahl has been an electronics enthusiast since he was a kid—he's always loved figuring out how things worked so he could try to build them for himself. He studied electronics and computer science at the University of Oslo, where he received a master's degree after building his own microchip. He then cofounded the company Intelligent Agent to develop sensors that allow robots to see through walls.

After a few years at Intelligent Agent, Øyvind set out on a mission to teach the world electronics. He gives workshops, develops courses, and writes about electronics and technology for a variety of outlets. He's posted hundreds of articles, tutorials, and videos on his blog (*http://www.build-electronic -circuits.com/*) and maintains Ohmify (*http://ohmify.com/*), a membership site that makes learning electronics fun and easy.

ABOUT THE TECHNICAL REVIEWER

John Hewes began connecting electrical circuits at an early age, moving on to electronics projects as a teenager. He later earned a physics degree and continued to develop his interest in electronics, helping school students with their projects while working as a science technician.

John has taught electronics and physics up to an advanced level in the United Kingdom and ran a school electronics club for children aged 11 to 18 years, setting up the website *http:// www.electronicsclub.info/* to support the club. He believes that everyone can enjoy building electronics projects, regardless of their age or ability.

BRIEF CONTENTS

CONTENTS IN DETAIL

2
MAKING THINGS MOVE WITH ELECTRICITY AND MAGNETS

3
HOW TO GENERATE ELECTRICITY

PART 2: BUILDING CIRCUITS

4
CREATING LIGHT WITH LEDS

69

5
BLINKING A LIGHT FOR THE FIRST TIME

6
LET'S SOLDER!   111

7
CONTROLLING THINGS WITH ELECTRICITY 131

8
BUILDING A MUSICAL INSTRUMENT 161

PART 3: THE DIGITAL WORLD

9
HOW CIRCUITS UNDERSTAND ONES AND ZEROS   187

10
CIRCUITS THAT MAKE CHOICES   213

11
CIRCUITS THAT REMEMBER INFORMATION 239

12
LET'S MAKE A GAME! 257

HANDY RESOURCES 281

INDEX 289

FOREWORD

There's something special about bringing a project to life that you read about in a book or that started as an idea in your head. And sometimes the simplest things are the most satisfying.

One of my favorite childhood projects was a mischievous little device made of a single resistor connected between the tip and ring of a telephone line. I used a piece of one-sided copper circuit board with rub-off symbols to lay out the design, and then I etched the unprotected copper away using ferric chloride in my basement. You could still use the phone normally to make outgoing calls, but anyone calling the house would receive a busy signal. This was the perfect way to make sure my parents didn't receive any phone calls from my teachers during dinner!

A few years later, I modified a garage door opener to open any door of the same brand. In normal operation, the passwords on the transmitter and receiver were manually set with a series of 10 DIP switches. If the transmission signal matched what the receiver was expecting, then the garage door would open. I replaced the switches on my transmitter with a common 555 timer IC, to generate a clock signal, and a 10-stage binary counter, a type of digital logic device, to automatically try every single possible combination (that's 2^{10} or 1,024 attempts). Within a few minutes of holding down the button, the correct password would be transmitted and the garage door would open! I never used my universal "brute-force" garage door opener for malicious purposes, but it reinforced my hacker mindset—solving problems with unconventional solutions, pushing the limits of technology, harming no one, and learning through constant questioning and experimentation. I also thought it was pretty cool to be able to modify an off-the-shelf device and make it do something the original designers probably never anticipated.

When I was much younger, I somehow ended up with a 6 V lantern battery and a spring from an adjustable lamp. I wondered, "What would happen if I connected the spring between the battery terminals?" So of course, I tried it. The spring got hotter and hotter until I freaked out, plucked it off the terminals, and threw it into the bathroom sink. I had created a short circuit by connecting the positive and negative terminals of the battery together, causing current to flow between them. I never looked at batteries and springs the same way again.

I remember trying to build my own alarm system for my bedroom door, sort of a low-tech version of the one you'll build in Chapter 1. I hung an old AM/FM radio from a hook on the back of my door, tuned it to static, turned the volume up to maximum, and "armed" it by connecting the sliding power switch to a wire I had attached to my wall. In theory, when the door opened, the wire would pull the switch and turn on the radio, blasting white noise at the intruder. That didn't happen. Instead, when my dad opened the door, the radio slid off the hook and crashed onto the floor. Back to the drawing board on that one!

These stories are meant to do one thing: inspire you to explore the wonderful, wild world of electrons—and this book is the perfect launch pad! Øyvind breaks down complex electronics fundamentals in an enjoyable, fun way. His passion for electronics and his love for teaching shine on every page. Starting with the basics and building up from there, you'll end up with the power to create bigger, better, faster, and more intelligent projects on your own. There's no better way to learn than by *doing*. So go ahead, turn the page and begin your adventure into all that electronics has to offer!

Joe Grand
Product Designer, Hardware Hacker, and Daddy
Portland, Oregon

ACKNOWLEDGMENTS

First of all, thanks to my father for explaining how things work based on practice instead of theory when I was a kid. His great explanations got me started in the world of electronics. Also, many thanks to my mother, who had to endure all those technical discussions around the dinner table.

Thanks to Jennifer Griffith-Delgado, Riley Hoffman, Tyler Ortman, and the rest of the team at No Starch Press—first of all for believing in me, but also for guiding me through the editorial process in such a good way. You have been a dream to work with!

Thanks to my technical reviewer, John Hewes, for finding my errors, challenging me in some areas, and making me think through some parts of the book a few extra times.

Finally, a special thanks to Garry Booth for the cover illustration, to Beth Middleworth for designing the layout and background illustrations, and to Riley once more, for drawing the technical diagrams. Those three really made this book come alive.

INTRODUCTION

Welcome to *Electronics for Kids*! This book will teach you how to make cool things by putting together the same parts that are inside televisions, electronic toys, radios, and all the other gadgets in the world. You'll build fun experiments, like a light powered by lemons, as well as useful (but still fun) projects, like an intruder alarm and a musical instrument.

You'll do more than just follow directions, however: you'll also learn how every component in each project works.

My hope is that when you know how those components work, you'll see how to create your own inventions by combining the components in different ways. Blinking a light is one of the first things I learned how to do with electronics. When I saw how that worked, a whole new world suddenly opened up to me. Since then, I've built robots, music players, miniature computers, and even a device that lets you see through a wall! With practice, you can build those things, too—and this book will teach you the basic skills you need to start the journey.

ABOUT THIS BOOK

When I was about 14 years old, I thought computers were cool, but I had no idea how they worked. They seemed magical, and I thought I'd never understand them or be able to build one. Luckily, my dad was an engineer, and he had a very good way of explaining things. When I asked questions, he showed me not only how things worked but also how I could build something similar myself.

I wrote this as the book I would have loved to have had as a kid, and I hope you enjoy it!

Who Should Read This Book

If you've ever looked at an electronic gadget and thought, "How does that work?" or "How can I make that?" as I did, then you're in the right place. Whether you're 8 or 100 years old, as long as you're curious and have a playful spirit, this book is for you.

How to Read This Book

I recommend you read this book in order, because every chapter builds upon concepts and skills covered in previous chapters.

Each chapter has at least one hands-on project. Build these projects! Electronics is a very practical skill, and reading about how a component works or what a project should do is different from experiencing it yourself. Just be sure to read a project in full before you dive into it so you understand the steps involved.

If you encounter problems as you build a project, don't worry: that happens to everyone at some point when working with electronics—even me. Just keep at it, study your circuit, and rewire the whole project if needed to get it working. When you've been battling to get a circuit working for a couple of hours, then suddenly find the error and your circuit works, you'll feel amazing! If you get stuck, grab a friend or family member and ask them to help out.

If there are parts of the book you don't understand right away, I recommend you keep on reading. Don't let details stop you. Come back to that particular topic later when you have some more projects under your belt.

What's in This Book?

As you work through this book, you'll build your knowledge of electronics gradually, starting with basic—but essential—information and simple circuits. After the basics, you'll build more complex circuits and meet components like resistors, capacitors, transistors, and integrated circuits. To see how the components work and to understand electronics in a practical way, you'll build fun projects in every chapter.

At the end of the book, you'll build one final, epic project: a game to play with your friends. By then, you'll have enough experience and knowledge to modify the game or even build a totally new game you invent yourself!

This book is divided into three parts. **Part 1: Playing with Electricity** is the foundation for the rest of the book. It's all about fundamental knowledge and how electricity actually works.

▶ **Chapter 1: What Is Electricity?** introduces the science behind electricity and describes the basic requirements for a circuit to turn something on.

▶ **Chapter 2: Making Things Move with Electricity and Magnets** shows you how you can move objects with electricity. In this chapter, you'll build a motor from scratch.

▶ **Chapter 3: How to Generate Electricity** describes how batteries and power plugs in the wall provide electricity. Of course, you'll build your own electricity sources, too!

Part 2: Building Circuits is where you'll really get your hands dirty. You'll meet some of the most important components in electronics, and you'll learn how to build both permanent and temporary circuits.

▶ In **Chapter 4: Creating Light with LEDs**, you'll build circuits on a breadboard for the first time to create a *prototype*, which is just a temporary circuit. You'll learn about resistors, light-emitting diodes (LEDs), and how to use those parts together.

▶ **Chapter 5: Blinking a Light for the First Time** shows how two new components, capacitors and relays, work. You'll even combine these with an LED to create a circuit that blinks a light.

▶ **Chapter 6: Let's Solder!** teaches you how to solder. With soldering, you can transform a circuit from a prototype to a proper device that will last for years to come.

▶ **Chapter 7: Controlling Things with Electricity** introduces the transistor, a component that lets a circuit control other circuits. You'll learn how transistors work and how to use them to build a touch sensor and a simple alarm clock.

▶ In **Chapter 8: Building a Musical Instrument**, you'll learn what an integrated circuit is and how circuits can make sound. You'll combine this knowledge to build a musical instrument.

Part 3: The Digital World introduces digital electronics, which almost all modern technology is based upon.

▶ In **Chapter 9: How Circuits Understand Ones and Zeros**, you'll learn about 1s and 0s, bits and bytes, and how to use them to communicate.

- **Chapter 10: Circuits That Make Choices** teaches you how to build smart circuits that use logic to make decisions. You'll build a secret code checker and learn how you can combine it with your intruder alarm.

- **Chapter 11: Circuits That Remember Information** shows how you can use logic gates to create circuits that remember information in a way similar to a computer. Then, you'll use this to create an electronic coin tosser.

- **Chapter 12: Let's Make a Game!** is dedicated to one large project. You'll get to show off your new skills by combining all the knowledge from the book to make a reaction speed game.

Finally, you'll find a **Handy Resources** appendix at the back of the book, which includes cheat sheets for figuring out component values, doing some essential electronics calculations, and so on. You'll learn about those concepts in detail throughout the book, but even electronics experts need a quick reference every now and then!

YOUR ELECTRONICS LAB

The wonderful thing about electronics projects is that your "lab" can be anywhere you want—it doesn't have to be a garage or workshop. All you need is a flat surface to work on, with enough room for your tools and components. Just gather the supplies to build your latest invention, and you're set.

Each project in this book includes a convenient list of the electronic components and tools needed to build it. Before you dig into a project, check its Shopping List to make sure you have all the materials. I've also created a complete list of all the components and tools you'll need for all the projects in this book, which you can find linked from the book's web page at *https://www.nostarch.com/electronicsforkids/*. This list should always have the most up-to-date part numbers and links to kits you can buy that contain all the necessary components.

Useful Supplies

Whether you're building the projects in this book or other projects on your own, there are a few supplies that will always come in handy:

- **A digital multimeter** (Jameco #2206061, Bitsbox #TL057, Rapid Electronics #55-6662) for testing connections and making sure a project is working correctly.
- **A pair of wire cutters** (Jameco #35482, Bitsbox #TL008)
- **A big spool of insulated wire** (Jameco #36792, Bitsbox #W106BK)
- **Electrical tape** to protect bare wires or fasten stuff.
- **9 V batteries**—nearly every project in the book uses one!
- **A bunch of LEDs** (Jameco #18041, Bitsbox #K033)
- **A bunch of resistors** (Jameco #2217511, Bitsbox #K017)
- **Safety glasses** to wear when snipping component leads, stripping wires, or soldering.

You can buy most of these from your local hardware store or from any online electronics retailer, like Jameco (*http://www.jameco.com/*), SparkFun (*http://www.sparkfun.com/*), or Bitsbox (*http://www.bitsbox.co.uk/*). Check out "Online Electronics Shops" on page 286 for more options.

You might also want to have a pair of scissors, some scrap paper, and pencils to take notes.

Safety First!

All the circuits in this book use a low voltage, and they're not dangerous to build and play with. That said, there are a few safety tips to keep in mind when using electronic components and tools:

- Wear safety glasses when trimming components or soldering.
- Use tools only for their intended purpose. Soldering irons are hot, and wire cutters are sharp—if used improperly, they can hurt you. If you're confused about how to use a tool, ask an adult for help.

- An adult should supervise younger children when they're working with small components, solder, tools, and so on to teach them how to use everything safely.

- Keep electronic parts out of reach of babies and very young children.

- Most projects in this book use batteries, but some do use power from a wall outlet. Follow the instructions for those circuits carefully. Never plug components directly into a power outlet, or you will get hurt.

Some projects do have steps you should take special care with, and I will clearly state that in the instructions with a warning, like this:

WARNING   *When you see this type of note, be careful with the step it talks about.*

Electronics is a safe hobby, though, so you won't see very many of these warnings. When you do see one, don't let it stop you from having fun. If you use common sense and follow the directions, you'll have nothing to worry about.

Now let's get started!

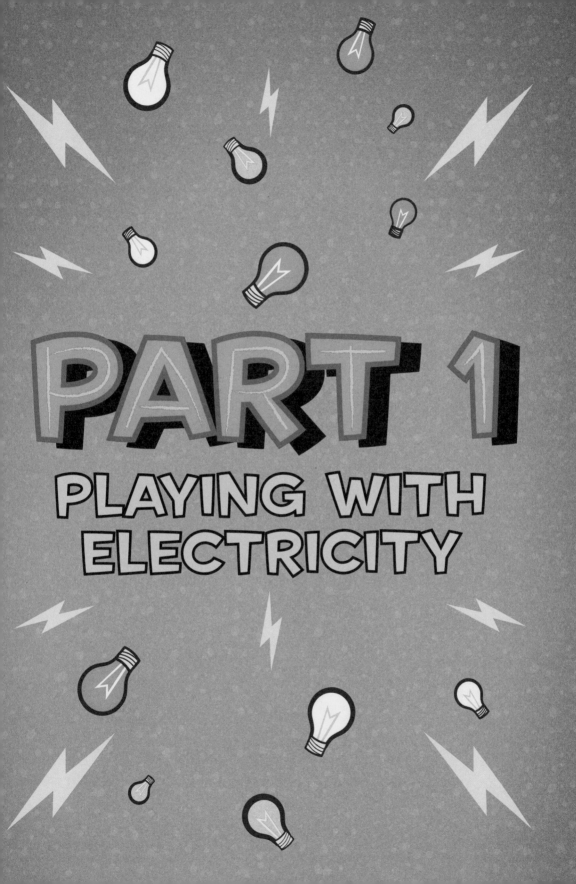

PART 1

PLAYING WITH ELECTRICITY

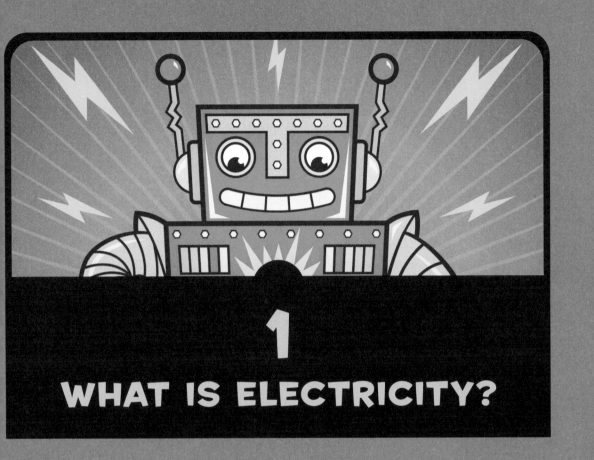

1
WHAT IS ELECTRICITY?

ush a button on a music player, and a song suddenly comes out of the speakers. Push a button on a TV's remote control, and your favorite shows come to life instantly. These wonders happen thanks to the magic of *electricity*, a type of energy that powers all the technology in your home. By the time you finish this book, you'll be an electronics wizard, and then you can try using your powers to build any invention you can imagine!

This book is all about understanding electricity and using it to make amazing things. In this chapter, we'll explore how electricity works, and then you'll build a complete electronics project: a burglar alarm that warns you if intruders have entered a room. Once you get the hang of using electricity, you can build all sorts of fun contraptions, like a musical instrument or a light-up game to play with your friends. In fact, you'll build these in this book.

PROJECT #1: TURN ON A LIGHT!

When you flip the light switch in a room, the bulb brightens right away. Let's look at how electricity makes that bulb shine, starting with a little experiment.

Shopping List

For this project, you'll need the following parts:

▶ **A standard 9 V battery** to power the circuit.

▶ **A small, incandescent light bulb** rated for 9 to 12 V (DigiKey #CM394-ND, Bitsbox #OP037, or a similar light bulb from a hardware store).

Step 1: Inspect the Light Bulb

Look closely at your light bulb; you should see a thin metal wire filament inside the glass. One end of this filament is connected to the metal side of the base, and the other end is connected to the metal contact on the bottom.

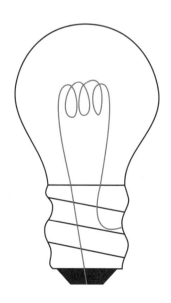

Step 2: Connect the Light Bulb to the Battery

Place your 9 V battery upright on a table. Take the light bulb and gently place it so that the bottom point touches one battery terminal and the metal side touches the other battery terminal. When both the bottom and the side are touching the battery, the bulb should light up.

Congratulations: you just generated light with electricity! The bulb lights because when you touch it to the battery contacts, electricity runs through the wire filament inside. The filament then heats and starts to glow, creating light.

HOW DOES ELECTRICITY LIGHT A BULB?

But *how* does electricity cause the wire to heat up, and why does the light turn on instantly? There are four concepts that combine to make that happen:

▶ Electrons

▶ Current

▶ Voltage

▶ Resistance

These fundamental concepts of electricity all depend on each other, and we'll explore them in this section.

What Is an Electron?

Everything you see around you is made of *atoms*, which are particles so small you can't see them without a special type of microscope. But atoms are made of even smaller particles, called *protons*, *neutrons*, and *electrons*.

Protons and neutrons form an atom's *nucleus* (its center), and electrons orbit the nucleus like planets orbiting the sun. Protons and electrons are both *electrically charged*: protons have a positive charge, and electrons have a negative charge. That's why the electrons stick with an atom in the first place. The positive and negative charges act like opposite sides of a magnet and attract each other.

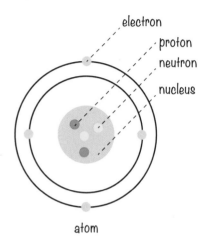

Certain materials are *conductive*, which means that if you apply energy to them (like the energy stored in a battery), the electrons will start moving from one atom to the next!

The filament inside your light bulb is made of a conductive metal, meaning it's full of electrons just waiting for a push to move them.

Voltage Pushes Electrons

When you attach a battery to the light bulb, you're applying a *voltage* across the filament inside. Voltage pushes electrons through the wire and is measured in *volts (V)*. The higher the voltage, the more electrons will flow through the wire.

Think of a wire like a tube filled with marbles: when you put a marble in on one side, a marble pops out on the other side at the exact same time, with no delay.

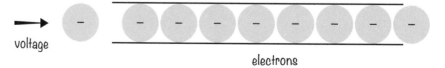

The more marbles you push in one side, the more pop out of the other. That's how electrons behave inside a wire, when a voltage is applied to them.

Current Flows

Current is the amount of electrons flowing through a wire, and it's measured in *amperes (A)*, which we usually shorten to *amps*. You might have also heard the word *current* used to describe a river, as in "This river has a strong current." That means there's a lot of water moving down the river.

Electrical current is similar: a strong current means there are a lot of electrons flowing through a wire. When you increase the voltage in a circuit, the current also increases.

Just as water flows downhill due to gravity, electric current flows from the positive battery terminal toward the negative battery terminal. Actually, the electrons themselves flow in the opposite direction, from the negative side of your battery to the positive side.* But when we talk about electrical current, we say that it flows from positive (+) to negative (–).

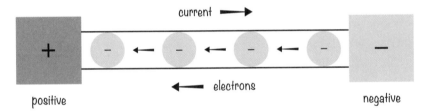

Resistance Reduces Current

Voltage pushes electrons to form a current, and *resistance* restricts the current. It's like playing with a garden hose: if you squeeze the hose, you add resistance to the flow of water so that less water comes out. But if you turn the tap more (like increasing the voltage), the pressure increases, and more water flows even though you're still squeezing the hose in the same way. Resistance in electricity works just like this, and it's measured in *ohms (Ω)*.

---

* The electron is a negative particle, but in some materials the current is made up of positive particles instead, and they flow in the opposite direction. So, at the atomic level, the particles can flow in either direction.

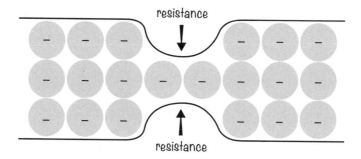

Now that you know about electrons, current, voltage, and resistance, I'll explain how they work together to turn on your light bulb.

Lighting the Bulb

The two ends of the wire filament inside your light bulb are connected to the outside of the bulb: one end is connected to the metal side of the base, and the other end is connected to the metal contact on the bottom. When you connect a battery to the light bulb, you create what's called a *circuit*. A circuit is just a closed path that allows current to flow from the positive terminal of your voltage source to the negative terminal.

The voltage on the battery pushes electrons through the circuit, including the filament inside your light bulb. The filament has resistance and restricts the current in your circuit. As the electrons struggle to make their way through the resistance of the filament, the filament becomes so hot that it starts to glow and generate light. For the battery to be able to push the electrons, there must be a *closed loop* going from the positive terminal on the battery to the negative terminal.

Electricity always needs a *closed circuit* to work. If you disconnect even one of the sides, the light bulb turns off right away! Let's look at circuits in a little more detail.

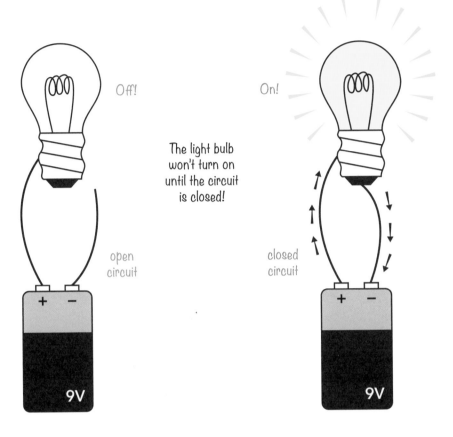

Off!

The light bulb won't turn on until the circuit is closed!

open circuit

On!

closed circuit

HOW IS A CIRCUIT LIKE A PIPE SYSTEM?

Let's continue to think about electricity by comparing it to water. Imagine a pipe system in a loop with a pump, and imagine the pipe is always totally filled with water. At one point, the pipe is narrower.

The pump is like a battery that gives power to a circuit. The narrow part of the pipe reduces the flow of water. This narrow pipe is the resistance. The amount of water that flows through the pipes is the current.

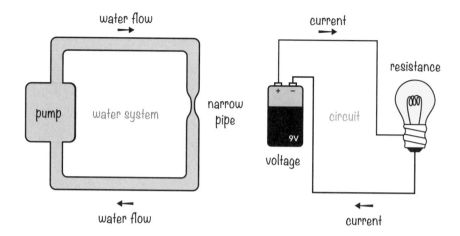

Now imagine that you could insert a measuring device somewhere in the pipe system that tells you how much water is flowing through it per second. Note that I'm talking only about how much water flows through one randomly selected point in the pipes, not the total amount of water in the pipes. This is how we'll talk about current in an electric circuit, too: it's the amount of electrons flowing through a certain point per second.

MEET THE SWITCH

When you look around your home, you probably see switches everywhere. You use them all the time to turn lights on and off! When the light in a room is turned on, it must be part of a closed loop because the bulb has current running through it. But what happens when you flip the switch off? Flipping the switch off is the same as disconnecting a wire in the loop: it stops current from flowing and turns the light off, just like the disconnected circuit we saw earlier.

What other switches can you find around you? You might find a switch that turns a computer on and off, a switch to ring a doorbell, a switch to determine whether a refrigerator door is open, and more.

Switches control electricity, and they're very simple devices. They connect two wires to close a loop or disconnect two wires to open a loop. Inside, a switch is just some pieces of metal that connect or disconnect.

When the switch is open, the light is off. When the switch is closed, the light turns on! It's very simple, but very useful. With only this knowledge, you can create some nifty circuits, and that's what we're going to do next.

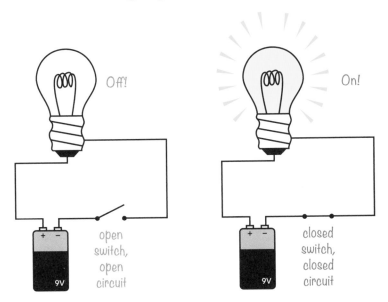

PROJECT #2: INTRUDER ALARM

In this chapter, we learned that electricity needs a closed circuit to make a circuit do anything interesting, and we've looked at how a switch works. Let's build a circuit with a switch!

You can build a switch out of a lot of different things— even a door. In this project, you'll turn a door into a gigantic switch and use it to build an intruder alarm that tells you when someone tries to enter the room.

To create the alarm, we'll attach some wires and aluminum foil to your door so that when the door is closed, your circuit is open and nothing happens. But when the door opens, the loop closes and a buzzer sounds to set off a red alert.

We'll hang an exposed wire down from above the door, place a strip of aluminum foil on top of the door, and connect each of these parts to a different side of the circuit. Then, when the door opens, the exposed hanging wire will touch the aluminum foil and close the loop so that the buzzer will sound.

Shopping List

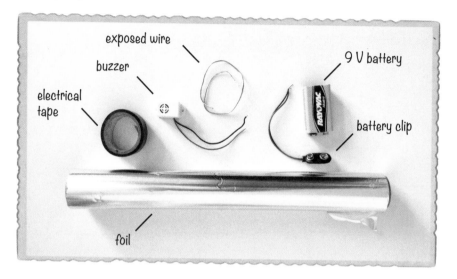

▶ **A buzzer** (Jameco #2173870, Bitsbox #ST016) that beeps. Buzzers come in both passive and active versions. Passive buzzers need an audio frequency input, while active buzzers need only a voltage. For this project, you need an active buzzer that works with 9 V.

▶ **A standard 9 V battery** to power the circuit.

▶ **A 9 V battery clip** (Jameco #11280, Bitsbox #BAT033) to connect the battery to the circuit.

▶ **Aluminum foil**

▶ **Exposed wire** (Jameco #2098478, Rapidonline.com #05-0320), like some soft electrical wires, an old steel guitar string, or something similar.

▶ **Tape** to fasten everything. You can use masking tape, electrical tape, or whatever you have.

Tools

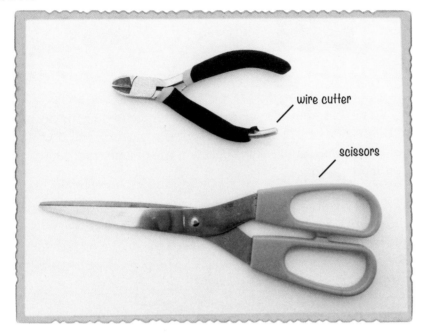

- **A wire cutter** (Jameco #35482, Bitsbox #TL008) to cut or remove the insulation from wire.
- **A pair of scissors** (optional) is useful for cutting the aluminum foil nicely.

TIP *If you want to make stripping wires even easier, you could buy a pair of actual wire strippers, like Jameco #78992, which are slotted so that you won't cut through the wire by accident.*

Step 1: Does the Buzzer Beep?

First, test the buzzer to see that it beeps. Hold the red wire from the buzzer to the positive terminal on your battery (marked +) and touch the black wire to the negative terminal on your battery (marked –).

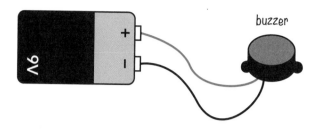

The buzzer should now make a loud, clear buzz or beep. If you disconnect one of the wires from the battery, the buzzer should stop making a sound because the circuit won't have a closed loop anymore.

NOTE *If your buzzer just made a click or didn't make any sound at all, you might have a passive buzzer. A passive buzzer can't create sound by itself, so you need an active buzzer for this project. The buzzer recommended in this project's Shopping List (page 12) should do the trick.*

Step 2: Prepare the Aluminum

Use a pair of scissors to cut a big, shiny strip of aluminum foil to go on the top of the door. Cut a straight piece of foil, about 1 inch wide and as long as the roll of aluminum foil is wide.

Step 3: Foil Your Door

Fasten the strip of aluminum foil on the top of the door by using a piece of tape on each side of the strip. The foil will act as a contact for the battery and buzzer wire.

Step 4: Prepare a Trigger Wire

Get a piece of exposed soft wire about 10 inches long. An *exposed wire* is a wire that doesn't have any plastic around it, as opposed to *insulated wire*, which is metal enclosed in plastic. Just find some wire that is already exposed, such as a steel string from a guitar, or use your wire cutters to snip a piece from the spool in the Shopping List (page 12). This is going to be your trigger wire.

NOTE *You could also use a wire cutter to remove, or strip, the plastic from insulated wires. If you want to do that, ask an adult for help!*

Step 5: Connect the Buzzer and Trigger Wire

Connect one side of the exposed trigger wire to the exposed metal end of the battery clip's black wire with some tape. Connecting two wires is easy. Here's how you do it: Pick up the two wires you want to connect and twist their ends together. Make sure the two pieces of metal are touching! Then wrap them inside the tape together.

Following the same process, connect the red wire from the battery clip to the red wire on your buzzer.

Step 6: Mount the Buzzer and Trigger Wire

Now, let's place the trigger wire and the buzzer above the door. First, tape the trigger wire onto the door frame above the door so that it's hanging in front of the door when the door is closed and lying on top of the door and the aluminum strip when the door is open.

Next, tape the buzzer to the door frame in such a way that the black wire can touch the aluminum foil on top of the door. Tape the black wire onto the foil so that the exposed part of the wire touches the foil.

Step 7: Add a Power Source

Place the battery on top of the door frame, close to the battery clip. Use some tape to hold it in place if necessary. Then connect the battery clip to the battery.

Once the battery is connected, your finished intruder alarm should look something like this:

Step 8: Stage an Intruder Alert!

Test the alarm by opening and closing the door. As the door opens, the exposed wire should hit the foil, causing the buzzer to sound a loud alarm. For a more realistic test, invite someone else to open the door instead!

Step 9: What If the Intruder Alarm Doesn't Work?

If the buzzer doesn't go off, you might need to adjust the position of the trigger wire a bit, just to make sure the wire touches the strip of aluminum foil when the door opens. If the trigger wire touches the foil just fine, try a different battery. If that doesn't work, you might need to retape your battery leads to their wires.

WHAT'S NEXT?

Now you know the basics of electricity—a current of electrons flows through wires and makes something happen, like lighting a light bulb or sounding an alarm. And you also know that to make the electrons flow through the circuit, you need a voltage source, such as a battery, and a closed loop. That's all you need to start tinkering with electronics!

What else can you think of to make with what you've learned? There are many other things that can be made into switches. For example, try making an alarm for your closet to keep nosy siblings or friends away from your personal stuff. Or how about making a silent alarm? Just replace the buzzer with a light bulb!

In the next two chapters, we'll look at how electricity is generated and how we can use electricity to make things move.

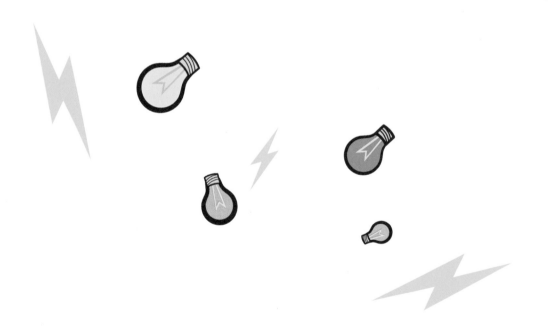

2
MAKING THINGS MOVE WITH ELECTRICITY AND MAGNETS

Big magnets attract small metal objects; small magnets stick to large metal objects. For example, refrigerator doors are usually big pieces of metal, so it's easy cover them with tiny, decorative magnets. You've probably seen magnets in cartoons, too: characters like to use giant horseshoe-shaped magnets to cause mischief. You can find magnets in nature or create them with electricity. A magnet created with electricity is called an *electromagnet*.

You can use an electromagnet to make things move, and you don't even have to be a superhero to do it! In fact, many things you see every day—like motors, loudspeakers, and the automatic doors in shops—work because electromagnets make something in them move.

An electromagnet is very easy to make, and in this chapter, you'll build an electromagnet that you can turn on and off with a switch. Then, you'll use an electromagnet to build your very own motor!

HOW MAGNETS WORK

Magnets have two poles, the *north pole (N)* and *south pole (S)*, and they're surrounded by a magnetic field.

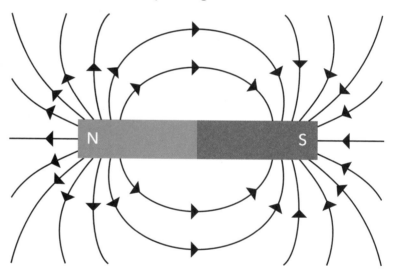

If you place two magnets side by side, the north pole of one magnet attracts the other magnet's south pole and repels that magnet's north pole. Try pushing two magnets together. If you don't force them, they should naturally attach to each other at their opposite poles. Now, try to force two of the same poles toward each other. That's harder, isn't it? Opposite poles are attracted to each other, and identical poles repel each other.

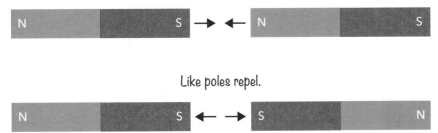

Unlike poles attract.

Like poles repel.

NOTE *Thin, flexible refrigerator magnets don't have two distinct poles. Instead they have many poles of opposite polarity next to each other, so it's harder to feel the magnets attract and repel.*

But magnets don't attract all materials. For example, plastic is unaffected by magnets. Try testing some metal objects around you!

TRY IT OUT:
FIND SOME MAGNETIC OBJECTS!

Take any magnet and place it over objects made out of different materials, such as:

▶ Aluminum foil

▶ A stainless steel spoon

▶ A soda can

▶ An iron nail

▶ A piece of metal jewelry

▶ A few different coins

Which objects does the magnet attract or stick to? You should find that the magnet attracts some metals, but not all metals. What happens with aluminum foil?

It turns out that some metals can turn into magnets if you apply a little electricity. That's where electromagnets come in.

MEET THE ELECTROMAGNET

When current flows through a wire, something strange happens: the current creates a magnetic field around the wire.

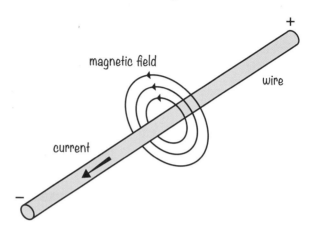

The magnetic field of one wire, however, is very weak. To make a stronger magnetic field, you need to run current through lots of wires placed next to each other. But you still need only a single wire: you can just wind that wire into many loops to make a coil, and then send a current through it. The magnetic fields from each loop in the coil overlap and combine to create a stronger magnetic field. If you wind your wire around a piece of iron—like a nail, a bolt, or a screw—you'll get an even stronger magnetic field.

All you have to do to create an electromagnet is connect a battery to the ends of the coiled wire, making a closed circuit. When current flows through the wire, the piece of iron it's wrapped around starts to behave like a magnet, with the south pole at one end and the north pole at the other end. Which pole is which depends on the direction of the current, as well as the direction of the coil windings. When you disconnect the battery, the current stops and the magnetic field disappears.

Building an electromagnet will help you start to understand how you can use electricity to make things like a loudspeaker in the real world, so let's make one! With enough current, enough wire, and the right circuit, you could build a supermagnet straight out of your favorite cartoon, but for now, we'll start with a small one.

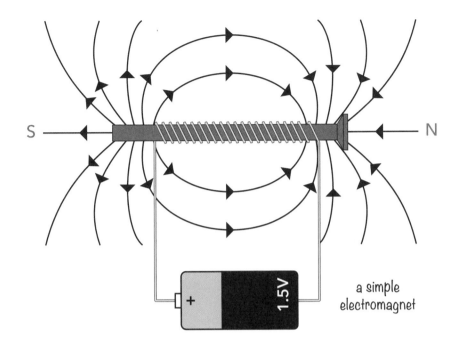

S   N

1.5V

a simple
electromagnet

PROJECT #3: CREATE YOUR OWN ELECTROMAGNET

You know the theory behind how to build your own electromagnet. But reading the theory isn't the same as making
something in real life, so it's time to have some fun!

You're going to build your own electromagnet with wire
and a bolt. All you need to do is to wrap the wire around the
bolt several times and connect the battery to the wire. To
make it easy to turn the electromagnet on and off, you'll also
add a switch to the circuit so that you can control whether or
not current flows through the wires.

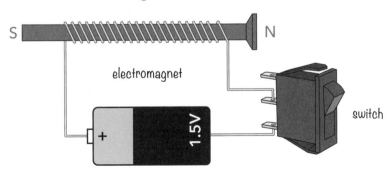

S   N

electromagnet

1.5V

switch

Shopping List

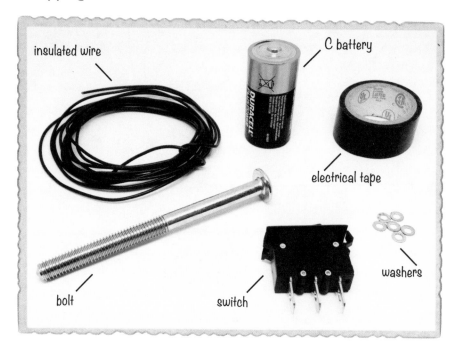

▸ **A 1.5 V alkaline (C) battery** (Jameco #2112428, Bitsbox #BAT040), like the big round ones used in older flashlights. Don't use a rechargeable battery or plug-in power supply.

▸ **Insulated solid-core wire** (Jameco #36792, Bitsbox #W106BK), about 7 feet. Standard hookup wire works fine.

▸ **Tape** to fasten everything. You can use masking tape, electrical tape, or whatever you have.

▸ **Washers or paper clips**, or other small metal objects that your electromagnet can lift.

▸ **A bolt** to wind the wire around. Choose a big one to make room for many turns with the wire. The bolt I used was 0.3 inches thick and 4 inches long.

▸ **A switch** (Jameco #581685, Bitsbox #SW018) to turn the electromagnet on and off.

Tools

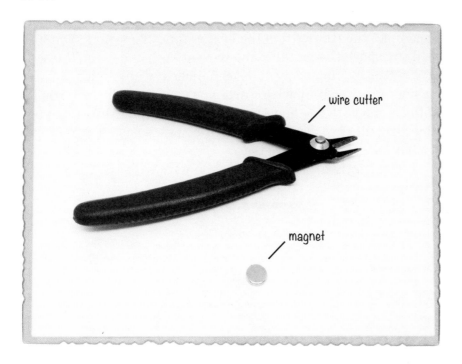

- ▶ **A wire cutter** (Jameco #35482, Bitsbox #TL008) to cut or remove the insulation from wire.

- ▶ **A standard magnet**

Step 1: Check Your Bolt

Your bolt is going to be the core of your electromagnet, making it stronger. But not all materials will work as an electromagnet's core! Most metal bolts should work, but if you're unlucky and find one that is made of nonmagnetic material, your electromagnet won't be very effective.

To check whether a bolt is okay to use in this project, just hold it close to any standard magnet. If the magnet attracts the bolt, then the bolt is a good one.

Step 2: Remove Insulation from One End of the Coil Wire

To connect the coil wire to the battery and the switch, you need to expose the metal of the wire at both ends. You'll use a wire cutter to strip away about 0.5 inches of insulation from the beginning of your wire. After you've wound the coil, you'll do the same with the end of your wire. Stripping wires can be a bit difficult if you've never done it before, so ask a parent or teacher for help to get started.

First, gently grasp the end of the wire with the cutters.

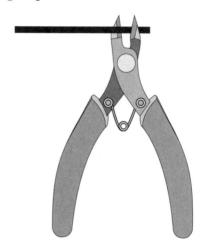

Apply just enough pressure with the wire cutter to cut the plastic around the wire, but not the wire itself. When you've cut through the insulation, your wire should look something like this:

Then, place the wire cutter in the cut you made. Squeeze the wire cutter enough to grip the loose plastic with the blades. Use the wire cutter to gently pull off the plastic without cutting into the metal of the wire.

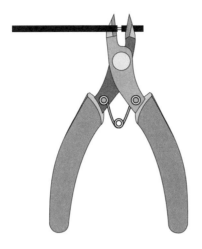

Now, you should have a wire with some exposed metal at the end, like this:

If stripping wires seems tricky in the beginning, don't worry: it becomes much easier with practice.

Step 3: Wind the Wire

Take the wire and wrap it around your bolt 50 to 100 times. Leave about 3 inches of each end of the wire hanging loose. Make sure you don't use all the wire; you'll need a piece of wire about 4 inches long in a later step.

Wrap the wire as tight as possible and tape the end to make sure the turns stay in place. We call this wound wire the *coil* of the electromagnet.

Repeat Step 2 to strip the insulation off the other end of your coil.

Step 4: Connect the Negative Battery Terminal to the Coil

Connect one end of the coil—it doesn't matter which—to the negative terminal of the battery. Fasten it to the battery with tape.

WARNING *Be sure you're using the recommended 1.5 V battery! Anything more powerful could send too much current through your coil, which could make both the battery and the coil hot enough to burn you.*

Step 5: Connect the Switch

In Chapter 1, I showed you how to build your own switch and described how you can use one to turn something on and off. Now, you're going to connect a prebuilt switch to your electromagnet to turn it on and off. A switch often has three *pins* that you can connect to.

On the switch in this project's Shopping List (page 24), pin 2 is the *common pin*, which is connected to either pin 1 or pin 3, depending on the position of the button. If the button is pushed toward pin 1, then pins 2 and 1 are connected. If the button is pushed toward pin 3, then pins 2 and 3 are connected.

Some switches have only two pins. In that case, the two pins are connected when the button is in one position, and not connected in the other—just like the switch you built in "Project #2: Intruder Alarm" on page 11.

Fasten the other end of the coil wire to pin 1 of the switch and make sure the button of the switch is pushed toward pin 3. Then, cut a brand-new piece of wire from your spool, about 4 inches long, and strip some insulation from both ends to expose the metal. Connect one end of the new wire to the positive battery terminal and one end to the middle pin of the switch. Use tape to make sure the wires are properly connected and stay in place.

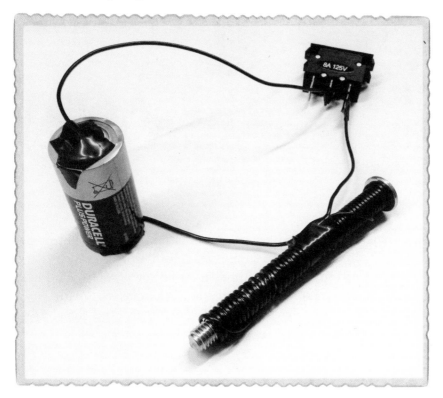

Step 6: Test Your Super Electromagnet

That's it for building the circuit! Now, let's test it. If you've connected everything correctly, your electromagnet should be off now.

First, find a good piece of metal to attract with your electromagnet. A small metal paper clip should do the trick, though I used a little pile of steel washers. Magnets won't attract all metals—for example, aluminum foil is not magnetic—so hold a regular magnet next to the metal you want to attract first to make sure it's magnetic.

Then, flip your switch and place your electromagnet close to your paper clip or whatever other metal object you're using. If you've found the *on* position, the bolt should pull the metal object toward it.

If nothing happens, press your switch into the other position; the bolt should start to pull the metal object now.

The electromagnet consumes a lot of power, so if you keep the switch flipped on for too long, your battery will drain quickly. You might also notice that the battery and the coil become hot. Try to limit the time your electromagnet is on to only a few seconds, and always disconnect the battery before you leave your circuit.

Step 7: What If the Electromagnet Isn't Working?

Make sure you used insulated wire to make the loops around the bolt. The wire must have some kind of insulating layer on the outside of the metal; otherwise, it won't work. The reason for this is that without the insulating layer, the current won't follow the wire loops around the bolt. Instead, they'll go through the bolt if the bolt is conductive or through to the neighboring wire if the loops of wire are touching. In either case, the current will function as if you had one thick wire.

Another possible problem is that your battery is dead. Try switching to a different battery that you're sure is working.

If you're sure you're using insulated wire and that the battery has power, check that the connections on the switch and battery are connected, as I described in Steps 4 and 5. If you're unsure, it might be a good idea to redo the connections.

MEET THE MOTOR

A wire with flowing current creates a magnetic field, as I described in "Meet the Electromagnet" on page 22. When powered, the coil from Project #3 will have a magnetic field with south and north poles, just like any other magnet. Like poles repel each other and opposite poles attract each other. So, if you put a magnetized coil of wire over a regular magnet with the same poles close to each other, the coil will try to twist itself around.

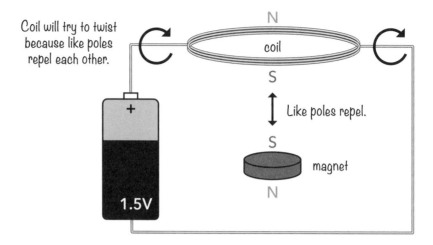

Coil will try to twist because like poles repel each other.

N

coil

S

Like poles repel.

S

magnet

N

+

1.5V

If you placed the wire coil on some kind of stand so that it could rotate freely over the magnet, it would flip back and forth without making a full spin. This is because when the coil has made a half spin, the opposite poles face and attract each other, which will force the coil in the opposite direction.

How can you make the coil continue to spin in one direction? You just need to find a way to disconnect the battery halfway around and turn the battery back on when the coil is back in its starting position. Then, here's what happens. The coil starts moving when it's powered and pushes the wire coil halfway through one round. Because you disconnect the battery halfway through, the existing motion keeps the coil moving forward. When it comes back to its original position, the battery gets reconnected and gives the coil another push forward, and it continues the same way.

Electric motors are based on this basic principle of magnetic poles attracting and repelling each other.

PROJECT #4: CREATE A MOTOR

In this chapter, you've built your own electromagnet, and you've learned how motors work. Now, it's time to combine these two concepts. In this project, you'll build your very own motor from scratch!

You'll use a magnet together with a coil of wire. The coil will spin, and this spinning coil is called the *rotor* of the motor. You're going to build the motor so that the rotor coil has current through it for only half of the spin. The magnet should push the electromagnet for half of the spin, and the rotor coil should continue around the second half of its spin with the energy it gets from the first push.

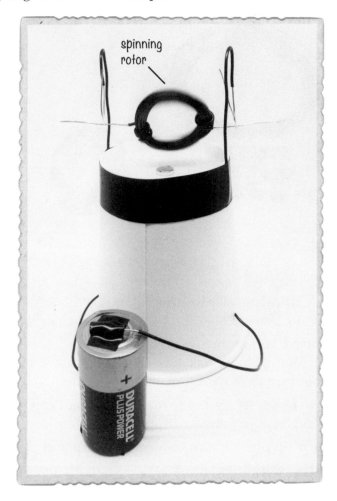

spinning
rotor

Shopping List

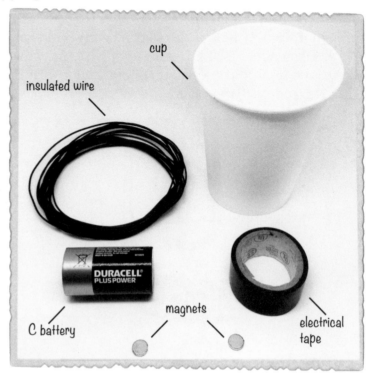

- **A 1.5 V alkaline (C) battery** (Jameco #2112428, Bitsbox #BAT040), like the big round ones used in older flashlights.

- **Insulated solid-core wire** (Jameco #36792, Bitsbox #W106BK), about 13 feet. The stiff insulated wire will be used both for the coil and to support the coil.

- **Tape** to fasten everything. You can use masking tape, electrical tape, or whatever you have.

- **A paper or plastic cup** to hold everything in place.

- **Two disc magnets** (Jameco #2181319, Bitsbox #HW145), the stronger the better.

WARNING   *Always keep small supermagnets like these away from babies and young children. These magnets are very dangerous if swallowed.*

Tools

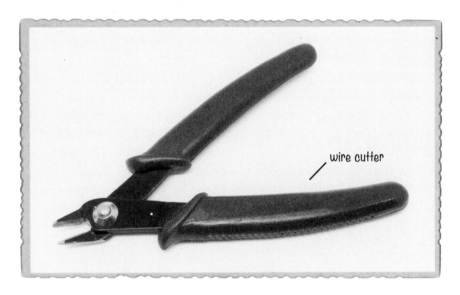

wire cutter

▶ **A wire cutter** (Jameco #35482, Bitsbox #TL008) to cut or remove the insulation from wire.

Step 1: Create the Rotor

First, we'll create a new coil of wire; this coil will be the rotor, or spinning part, of your motor. To create the rotor, first take your spool of wire and strip the insulation from about 1.5 inches of the free end. Then, wind the wire around the battery.

If you buy the wire I recommend in this project's Shopping List (page 34), try making around 30 windings; if you use thinner wire, wind it more. The point is to make the coil as magnetic as possible, without making it too heavy. More windings make the rotor more magnetic, but also heavier.

Carefully slide your coiled wire off the battery. Gather the windings into a loop and wrap the ends of the wire around your loop a few times on each side so that the coils stay together. Cut your loop from the spool of wire, leaving the other end about 1.5 inches long. Then, remove the insulation from this end, too, so that the metal inside is exposed. If you're using wires with plastic insulation, you can use a wire cutter, as described in Step 2 of Project #3 (page 26).

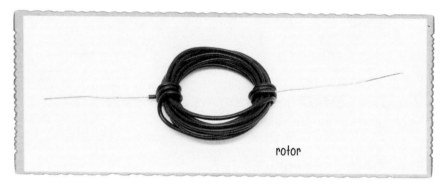

rotor

Step 2: Build the Motor's Structure

Set your coil aside for now and take out your paper cup. Punch a hole in one side of the cup about 0.4 inches from the top and another one about 0.4 inches from the bottom. Pull a piece of the stiff wire around 8 inches long through these two holes. Then, do the same on the other side of the cup. Turn the cup upside down, remove the insulation from the ends of both wires, and tape the wires to the cup to ensure they stay in place.

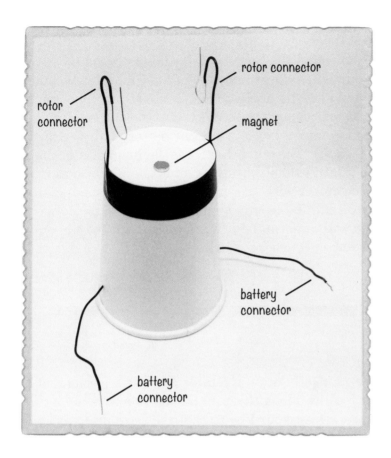

The ends that are now on the bottom will connect to the battery, and the top ends are going to make up the connection to the rotor and support it. Bend the top ends of the two wires into two U-shapes that can hold the rotor. Make sure the bottom part of each U has exposed metal so that it will touch the exposed wires of the rotor. This U-structure will be the battery's connection to the rotor.

Step 3: Place the Magnets

Place one magnet on top of the cup. Then place one magnet inside the cup so that the two magnets stick to each other through the cup. Place your rotor into the U-structure and adjust the position of the magnets to make sure they are at the center, just under the coil.

Step 4: Reinsulate Part of the Coil

If you connected the battery now, the motor wouldn't work. With your coil rotor attached, you'd see movement, but the rotor would just be pushed back and forth in opposite directions because it's always connected to the battery. You need a way to disconnect the coil from the battery halfway through so that it's first pushed away from the magnet and then released until it has spun the rest of the way around. Then, it can reconnect with the magnet and get pushed again, and so on. You can make this happen by insulating the wire on one side with a permanent marker. Do this on only one arm of the rotor.

wire insulated with permanent marker

no insulation

Lay your coil flat on the table and use a permanent marker to draw along the wire on one side to make it nonconductive. Draw your line so that the rotor disconnects from the battery when the loop lies horizontally above the magnet.

Step 5: Rev Up Your Motor

Let's get that motor running! Connect the battery by taping the two wires to the positive and negative terminals.

wire connected to the positive battery terminal

Now, place the rotor into the U-structure. The motor should start spinning. You might need to give it a little push. It won't run any cars, but if it works, then you definitely just made something move with electricity. Congratulations!

The motor is running!

Step 6: What If the Motor Doesn't Work?

Can you see any movement? If you're very lucky, it'll work right away, but you'll most likely need to make some adjustments. Here are some places to start:

1. Make sure your coil is placed so that it starts with the exposed wire—that is, not the part you covered with the marker—touching the exposed wire of the U-shaped structure. That way, when you connect the battery, the coil becomes magnetic.

2. Figure out which way the battery should be connected. You might find that the rotor spins better in one direction than the other, so try to connect the battery the other way around to see what's best for your motor.

3. If your coil is a bit too heavy, the magnetism won't be enough to push the coil all the way around the loop. Try unwinding a few loops to make the coil lighter.

4. You might need to adjust the position of the magnets under your rotor. They should be as centered as possible.

If your motor still doesn't run, your rotor may just need a little push to get started. Try tapping it lightly with your finger to see whether that unleashes a speed demon.

WHAT'S NEXT?

In this chapter, you've learned that magnets can be created by winding a wire around a bolt and connecting it to a battery, and you've tested this by building your own electromagnet. At the end, you learned how electric motors work, and you even built one for yourself. You really got things moving!

Now, take that knowledge and explore electricity a little further. Try adding even more magnets under the rotor of your motor. Then, wind a rotor coil that is twice as big or even bigger. You can create a much larger structure for the motor. How fast can you make your motor go?

So far, you've only used electricity, but you can actually generate it, too. In the next chapter, you'll learn a couple of different ways to generate electricity, and you'll be playing around a bit more with magnets.

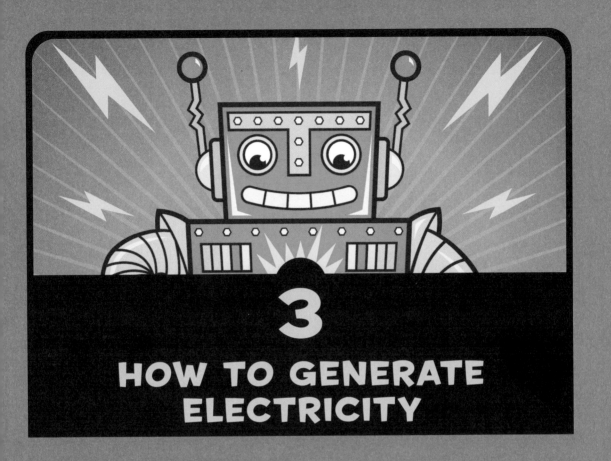

3

HOW TO GENERATE ELECTRICITY

Chapter 1 described why you need a closed loop to get current flowing through a circuit, and Chapter 2 showed you how to build your own electromagnet and motor. The projects in those chapters used electricity from a battery, but in this chapter, you'll make your own electricity sources!

Specifically, you'll learn how to build your own generator, which creates electricity from movement, and your own
battery, which creates electricity through chemical reactions.
These are two of the most common ways to obtain electricity.

GENERATING ELECTRICITY WITH MAGNETS

When you run current through a wire, it creates a magnetic
field around the wire, but there's another connection between
electricity and magnetism. You can also create electricity
using a wire and a magnet!

A Changing Magnetic Field Creates Electricity

If you move a magnet back and forth over a wire connected in
a closed loop, you'll create a current in the wire. Moving the
magnet changes the magnetic field around the wire, and the
changing magnetic field pushes the electrons through the wire.

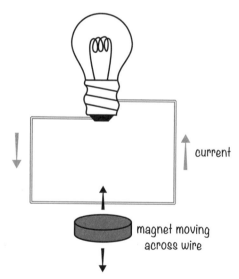

current

magnet moving
across wire

If you stop moving the magnet, the current also stops—
even if the wire is still within the magnetic field—because the
magnetic field is no longer changing.

If you connect the two ends of the wire to a light bulb and create a closed loop, then the current can flow. Unfortunately, however, the current created by moving a magnet over a single wire doesn't provide enough energy quickly enough to actually light the bulb. To light a bulb, or to power anything else, you need to find a way to generate more *power*, which is the amount of energy produced in a certain time.

How Does a Generator Work?

A *generator* is a device that turns movement—such as the movement of a magnet over a wire—into electricity. To create more power with a wire and a magnet, you can wind that wire into a coil. The coiled wire acts like a group of wires, and when the magnetic field passes through it, a current flows through each coil, creating more power than you could with a straight wire.

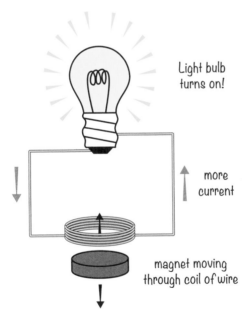

Light bulb turns on!

more current

magnet moving through coil of wire

CREATING ELECTRICITY FROM WATER OR WIND

If you place a coil in a magnetic field and rotate the coil with a handle, you're converting your own movement into electricity. If you replaced the handle with a water wheel and placed it into a stream of water, the water would push the wheel so that the coil would rotate in the magnetic field and create a current. This is how some power plants generate electricity! The power plant just lets water run through a wheel that's connected to a generator. Then this electricity is transferred, through power lines, to the power outlets in people's houses.

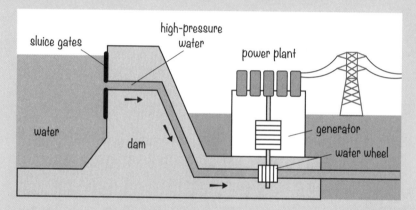

You can make electricity out of other natural forces in the same way. For example, to create electricity out of wind, you can connect the coil to a windmill so that when the wind blows, it rotates the coil.

MEET THE MULTIMETER

You can measure exactly how much energy a simple generator creates with a basic *multimeter*. Multimeters are handy when building any circuit because they can measure a lot of different values, including resistance, current, and voltage.

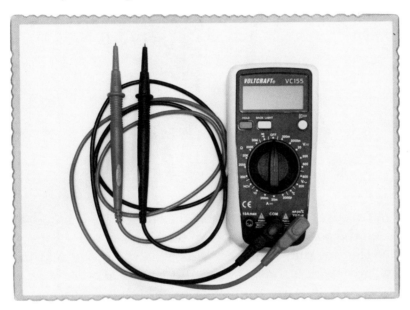

The red lead is the positive lead, the black lead is the negative lead, and the big dial in the middle lets you tell the multimeter what to measure. If you're having problems with a circuit, measuring the voltage at key points in your circuit is one practical way to figure out what's wrong.

How to Measure Voltage

To measure voltage with a multimeter, first turn the dial to one of the V options. (In this book, I'll tell you which setting to choose, but in your own projects, pick one that has a number higher than the highest voltage you expect to see in your circuit.) Then, at the bottom of the multimeter, connect the black lead to the COM socket and the red lead to the V socket. Finally, place one lead on each side of the part you want to measure the voltage across.

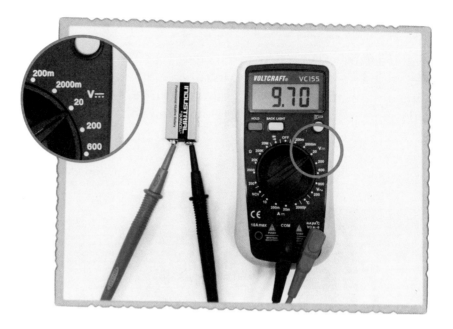

In this example, the meter is measuring the voltage between the positive and negative terminals of a 9 V battery. Notice that my dial is turned to 20 V, in the range showing a V with a straight-line symbol. But there's another V on the multimeter with a wavy line next to it. Let's look at what these symbols mean.

What Are AC and DC?

How you set your multimeter depends on whether you want to measure the voltage from a battery or a generator. A battery has a positive and a negative side, but a generator doesn't! A generator has two wires that alternate between being positive and negative. This is because when one side of the magnet moves past the coil, current in the coil flows in one direction, and when the other side of the magnet moves past the coil, current flows in the other direction.

When the current direction switches like that, we call it *alternating current (AC)*; when the direction of the current stays the same all the time, we call it *direct current (DC)*.

Usually, you'll find these symbols on your multimeter to indicate the AC and DC ranges of measurement:

AC   DC

You need to set the multimeter to measure either AC or DC to get the correct reading. For example, batteries have a DC voltage.

PROJECT #5: MAKE A SHAKE GENERATOR

Grab your multimeter—this project will show you how to make a generator and measure its voltage. One quick way to create a simple generator is to manually move a magnet back and forth inside a coil. In this project, you'll put a magnet inside a tube and wind a coil around the tube. When you shake the tube, the magnet should move back and forth inside the coil and create a voltage.

Shopping List

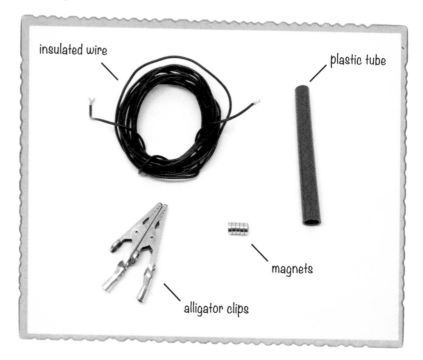

- **Insulated solid-core wire** (Jameco #36792, Bitsbox #W106BK), about 9 feet. Standard hookup wire works fine.
- **A small plastic tube**, such as an old pen.
- **Five disc magnets** (Jameco #2181319, Bitsbox #HW145) stacked to form a magnet rod.
- **Two alligator clips** (Jameco #256525, Bitsbox #CN262) to connect the multimeter to the coil.

Tools

- **A multimeter** to measure the voltage of your generator. The multimeter should be able to measure very low AC voltages, down to 0.01 V or less. Suitable multimeters are Jameco #2206061, Bitsbox #TL057, or Rapid Electronics #55-6662. These multimeters are a bit more expensive than the cheapest ones, but they will serve you for many years to come.

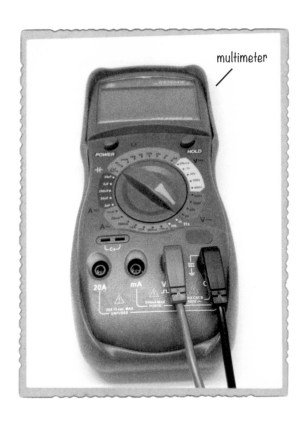

multimeter

Step 1: Prepare Your Tube

Find a tube that's big enough to let the magnets slide easily back and forth. If you're using a pen, disassemble the pen and make sure your magnets fit inside the tube.

Step 2: Wind Your Coil

Wind about 50 turns of wire around the middle of your tube. After winding, make a simple knot with the two ends to keep your coil together. Then, strip the insulation from the two wire ends, as shown.

Step 3: Connect the Multimeter

Connect the multimeter to both ends of the coil using alligator clips and set the multimeter to measure AC. Choose the lowest AC voltage setting available.

Step 4: Shake That Thing!

Next, put the magnets inside the tube. They should fit inside without coming apart.

Holding the tube and multimeter leads in your hand, place one finger on each side of the tube so that the magnets don't fall out. Then, shake it like you mean it!

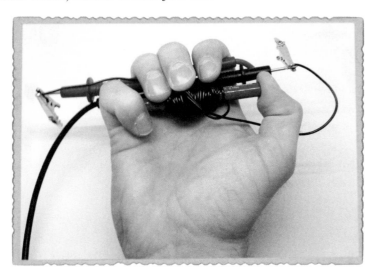

Observe the voltage value on the multimeter. How much voltage do you get? I was able to get only 0.02 V from my generator, so it's not very powerful.

Step 5: What If There's No Voltage?

If you can't measure any voltage from your generator, first check that your multimeter leads are connected well to the exposed coil wires. If you still don't see a voltage higher than 0 V, make sure your multimeter is set to measure really low voltages; my dial was turned to 2 V AC. You won't get a high voltage from this simple generator, so if the multimeter isn't on the lowest setting possible, it will keep reading 0 V. Note that not all multimeters are able to measure such low voltages.

This generator isn't very powerful right now. How can you make it more powerful? Try to increase the voltage from the generator by shaking it faster, adding more loops of wire to the coil, or using a more powerful magnet.

NOTE *Standard hookup wire is a bit bulky; even 50 turns take up a lot of space! If you want to get a lot more turns, try using* magnet wire *instead. It's really thin wire with a thin layer of insulating coating.*

TRY IT OUT:
USING A MOTOR AS A GENERATOR

A motor already has a magnet and a coil of wire that can rotate in the magnet's magnetic field. If you rotate the rotor with your hand, you can generate a voltage on the motor's wires.

You could create a generator by reversing the motor you built in Chapter 2, but the power you'd get from it would be too small to measure. Instead, try to find an old motor from a computer fan or a radio-controlled toy car that you don't want to play with anymore. Then, set your multimeter to a low-voltage DC range, such as 2 V DC. Attach the multimeter leads to the motor wires, just as you did with the shake generator, and turn the rotor with your fingers. Some motors have internal circuits that control the motor, and those circuits can prevent the electricity generated inside the motor from going out to the wires. But if you're lucky and find a motor that doesn't have such circuits, you should see a reading on the multimeter. Try a low-voltage AC range on your multimeter if you see nothing with DC.

HOW DO BATTERIES WORK?

I've shown you how to generate electricity manually, but that doesn't explain how you've powered circuits up to this point in the book. You've been using batteries, and in this section, we'll look at what lets those batteries create electricity.

What's Inside a Battery?

To create a battery, you need three things:

▶ A positive electrode

▶ A negative electrode

▶ An electrolyte

An *electrode* is a wire that is used to make contact with something nonmetallic, like the inside of a battery. An *electrolyte* is a substance that can release or gain electrons.

Here's how these three pieces fit inside a typical battery:

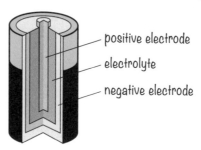

positive electrode

electrolyte

negative electrode

You can actually make your own battery by using a simple nail for one electrode and a copper wire for the other. Stick both into a lemon, and the lemon juice is your electrolyte.

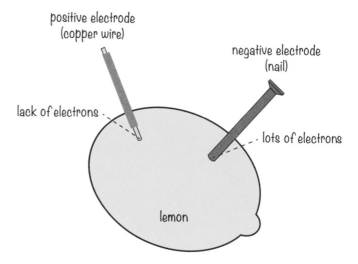

positive electrode
(copper wire)

negative electrode
(nail)

lack of electrons

lots of electrons

lemon

The copper wire becomes the positive terminal of the battery, and the nail becomes the negative terminal.

The Chemistry Behind Batteries

When you combine the lemon, the copper wire, and the nail, two chemical reactions happen: one between the lemon juice and the nail, and another between the lemon juice and the copper wire. In the first reaction, electrons build up on the nail; in the second, electrons leave the copper wire. The nail gets too crowded with electrons, and the copper wire ends up with too few. Electrons don't like to be in crowded places, so the electrons on the nail want to go over to the copper wire to even things out. But the chemical reactions with the lemon juice are pushing the electrons the other way.

Now, what do you think will happen if you connect a light bulb between the nail and the copper wire? The electrons on the nail really want to get to the copper wire, so they'll take the easiest path they can find, and when you create this closed-loop circuit, they flow from the nail to the copper wire through the light bulb. Recall that current is just electrons flowing in a wire; if you have enough current flowing through the light bulb, it lights up!

After a while, the chemical reactions in the battery stop. When this happens, the battery is dead. Some batteries can be recharged when they die, while others must be thrown away. The materials chosen for the electrodes and electrolyte determine whether the battery can be recharged or not.

The batteries you buy in the store are not made of lemons, of course! Modern batteries are made from different materials, and scientists are always looking for new ways to create batteries that have more energy, while being small and lightweight.

What Determines a Battery's Voltage?

The materials used for the electrodes and electrolyte determine the voltage you get from a battery, but the size of the electrodes and the amount of electrolyte don't matter when it comes to voltage.

To create higher battery voltages, several battery cells are connected in *series*. Connecting two battery cells in series means that you connect the positive side of one battery to the negative side of the other. The two unconnected terminals become the bigger battery's new positive and negative terminals, and the resulting voltage is the sum of the voltages from the two batteries. For example, in a standard 9 V battery, you have six 1.5 V battery cells, as shown. Notice that the connectors on the outside are attached to just two terminals.

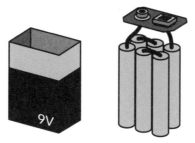

PROJECT #6: TURN ON A LIGHT WITH LEMON POWER

You can make a battery out of many different things; for example, in "What's Inside a Battery?" on page 55, I showed you how a lemon battery might work. In this project, you'll learn how to build a lemon battery of your own and power a light with it.

WARNING   *When you're finished with this project, throw the lemons away. The chemical reactions that happen with the nail and copper wire will leave the lemons unsuitable for eating.*

Meet the LED

A lemon battery can't create a lot of electricity, so you need to connect the battery to something that needs very little power to see the effect. Most light bulbs need more power than you'll generate in this project, so let me introduce a component called a *light-emitting diode*, or *LED*.

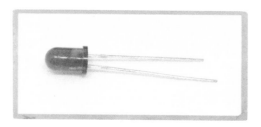

This little electronic component gives off, or *emits*, light when you apply a little bit of power to it. LEDs come in many colors: red, green, yellow, blue, and more. You'll learn more about this component in Chapter 4, and you'll use LEDs a lot in this book. For now, you're just going to use an LED to see the power generated by your lemon battery.

Shopping List

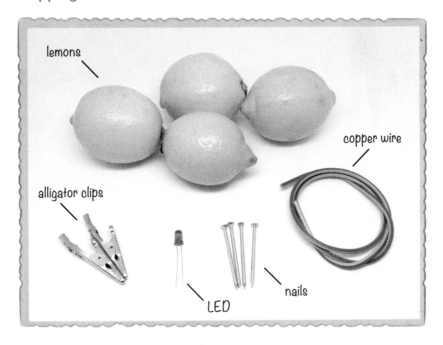

▶ **Four lemons** or one lemon cut into four pieces.

▶ **24 inches of copper wire** (any copper wire will do, but it's important that the wire be copper).

▶ **Four galvanized nails** (most common nails for outdoor projects are galvanized).

▶ **Two alligator clips** (Jameco #256525, Bitsbox #CN262) for connecting the LED.

▶ **A standard LED** (Jameco #333973, Bitsbox #OP002 for just this one, or Jameco #18041, Bitsbox #K033 for a variety pack). You'll need several LEDs for the projects in this book, so order at least 10 or a variety pack.

Tools

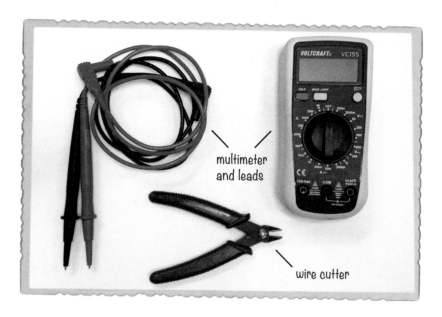

multimeter and leads

wire cutter

▶ **A wire cutter** (Jameco #35482, Bitsbox #TL008) to prepare the copper wire.

▶ **A multimeter** (Jameco #2206061, Bitsbox #TL057, Rapid
Electronics #55-6662) to see whether your battery is working correctly.

Step 1: Prepare Your Wires

First, cut your copper wire into four 6-inch lengths. Strip
about 1 inch of insulation from both ends of each wire. These
will become the electrodes.

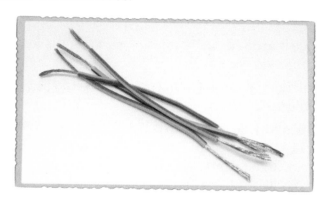

Step 2: Insert Electrodes into a Lemon

Roll and squeeze a lemon so that you break up the small juice packets inside it, but not enough to break the skin. Then, use a nail to make one hole in one end, push a copper wire into that hole, and push the nail into the other end, as shown. This is the first lemon battery!

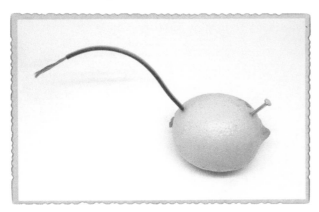

Get your multimeter, set it for DC voltage measurement, and test your lemon battery now. Place the positive test lead on the copper wire and the negative test lead on the nail. If everything works correctly, you should see a voltage of around 1 V on your multimeter.

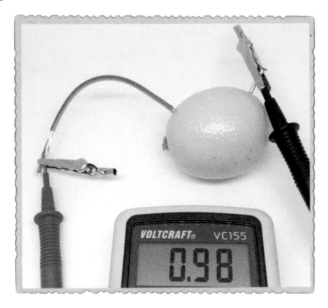

Step 3: Create Four Lemon Batteries

Even if you get 1 V out of your lemon, that's not enough to light an LED. Let's create several lemon batteries so we can get more electricity!

Just repeat the process described in Step 2 for the other lemons; each will become a battery. (If you don't have four lemons to spare, you can cut one lemon into four pieces.) Now you should have four lemon batteries.

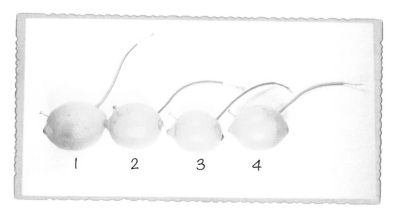

Step 4: Connect the Lemons in Series

To get a higher voltage with your lemon batteries, you'll need to connect them in series. To connect two lemons in series, you just connect the positive side of one lemon to the negative side of another. Remember, the copper wire is positive, and the nail is negative.

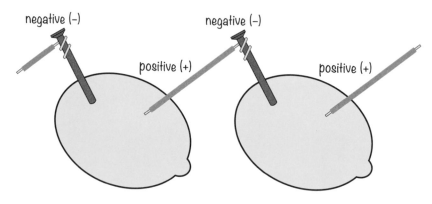

To wire four lemons in series, just repeat that process a couple more times. Line your lemons up in a row with the copper wires pointing to the right and number the lemons from 1 to 4, beginning from the left. Connect the copper wire from lemon 1 to the nail in lemon 2. Twist the wire onto the nail so that the metals connect without coming apart.

Connect the copper wire of lemon 2 to the nail in lemon 3, and connect the copper wire from lemon 3 to the nail in lemon 4. This should give you a row of four lemons, with an unconnected nail on lemon 1 and an unconnected copper wire on lemon 4. These are the positive and negative terminals for your big lemon battery, respectively.

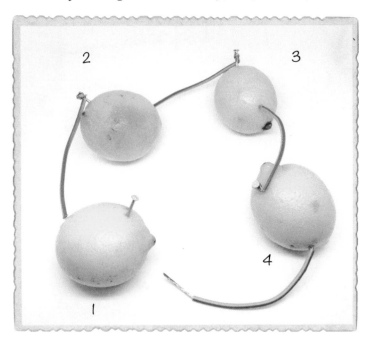

When you connect batteries in series, you can add their voltages to find your total. Four 1 V lemon batteries should give you 4 V. If you have a multimeter, measure the voltage between the two ends to see whether everything is connected. You should get a voltage of around 3.5 to 4 V.

Step 5: Test Your Lemon Battery

Let's connect the LED to the lemons! Connect the long leg
from the LED to the copper wire, and connect the short leg
to the nail, as shown. The LED should now light up.

Lemons aren't super powerful batteries (you'd never see anyone with a lemon connected to their computer, for example), so your LED will probably be very dim. After you finish building your lemon-powered circuit, turn off the light in your room, and you should see the LED glow.

Remember, when you're finished with your lemon battery, throw the lemons away—don't eat them!

TRY IT OUT:
MORE FOOD BATTERIES!

When you're done making lemon batteries, test to see whether you can make batteries out of other fruits or vegetables. For example, what about a potato battery? Are you able to get more voltage, or is it the same as the voltage from the lemon?

Step 6: What If Your Lemon Light Doesn't Work?

If you can't see light from your LED, even in a dark room, check to see whether your LED is connected the right way. The long leg should be connected to the positive side of the battery, which is the copper wire.

Make sure the lemons are connected to each other only through the wires and nails. For example, if your lemons are sitting in a puddle of lemon juice, they could be connected through that. Just dry them off and move them somewhere else. Next, check that the copper wires are properly connected to the nails and that the nails and copper wires are actually touching the juice inside the lemons. Also, check that the nails and copper wires are not touching each other inside any of the lemons.

If the circuit still doesn't work, disconnect all the lemon batteries from each other. Then, use a multimeter to check that each lemon battery has some voltage. Connect two lemons in series, and check that you see a higher voltage. Connect the third lemon, and check that the voltage has increased again. Then, connect the fourth lemon and check that you have even more voltage.

If you see a voltage but the LED doesn't light, then you probably just need some more power. Get another lemon or two, create some more batteries, and connect them in series with the rest.

WHAT'S NEXT?

In this chapter, you learned how to create your own electricity from magnetism and chemical reactions. You made your own shake generator, and you built a lemon battery to power an LED.

If you want to explore generators even more, I suggest trying to find a *dynamo* from an old bike. Unlike the generator you built in this chapter, a dynamo is a generator that gives you a DC voltage, like a battery, and dynamos are commonly used to power headlights on bikes. Cut some windmill blades out of some stiff cardboard or plastic, connect them to the dynamo, and see whether you can harvest energy from the wind.

You've now met a few electronic components, including switches, LEDs, and motors. In the following chapters, you'll learn about even more components and graduate to building some real electronic circuits, like lights that blink, a touch-sensitive switch, and even your own electronic musical instrument!

PART 2
BUILDING CIRCUITS

4

CREATING LIGHT
WITH LEDS

ights, especially LEDs, are used all the time in electronics. Sometimes, they're just simple indicators that show whether a device is on or not, but they can also be part of more complicated devices, like computer displays. In fact, some displays are actually made up of thousands of tiny LEDs.

In this chapter, you'll learn how two of the most common basic components in electronics work: the resistor and the LED. I'll show you how to kill an LED, but don't worry: you'll learn how to use resistors to keep LEDs alive, too. In this chapter's projects, you're also going to start using a new tool, called a *breadboard,* to connect circuits. Many projects in this book use breadboards, and you can also use them to build a lot of cool projects on your own.

MEET THE RESISTOR

Recall that resistance restricts current from flowing freely in a circuit. A *resistor* is a component that adds resistance to a circuit. The more resistance your circuit has, the less current will flow through it.

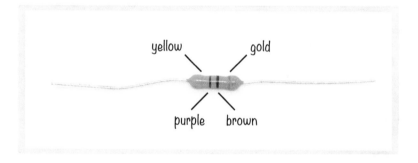

Resistor Color Codes

When you look at a resistor, you'll notice that it has several colored bands. These colors tell you the value of the resistor. Resistance is measured in *ohms,* but when we write about it, we'll use an *omega* symbol, Ω, for short. More ohms means more resistance.

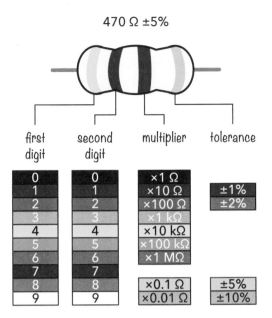

470 Ω ±5%

first digit	second digit	multiplier	tolerance
0	0	×1 Ω	
1	1	×10 Ω	±1%
2	2	×100 Ω	±2%
3	3	×1 kΩ	
4	4	×10 kΩ	
5	5	×100 kΩ	
6	6	×1 MΩ	
7	7		
8	8	×0.1 Ω	±5%
9	9	×0.01 Ω	±10%

Most resistors have four color bands. From the left, the first band gives the first digit of the resistance value. In this example, the first band is yellow, so the first digit is 4. The second digit is given by the second band, which is purple for 7. Together, this gives us the base value of 47. Next we multiply 47 by the value of the third band—the *multiplier*. In this example, the brown band stands for 10 Ω, so we multiply 47 by 10:

$$47 \times 10 \text{ Ω} = 470 \text{ Ω}$$

NOTE   *If a resistor has five bands instead of four, then the first three bands are digits, and the fourth is the multiplier.*

But the actual resistance of a resistor usually won't match the value written on it! That sounds a bit crazy, right? It's hard for manufacturers to create resistors with a very exact resistance value, so instead, they make sure the resistors are somewhere around that value and tell you how far off the real value could be.

This is where *tolerance* comes in. Our example resistor is labeled 470 Ω with a tolerance of 5 percent. This means that the resistor's real resistance could be any value 5 percent higher or 5 percent lower than 470 Ω. Because 5 percent of 470 is around 24, the real resistance could be anywhere between 446 Ω and 494 Ω.

Usually, the three bands that tell you the resistance value are grouped together, and the band that tells you the tolerance is spaced a bit farther away. But sometimes the bands are so close that it's hard to see which three bands give the resistance. Fortunately, the fourth band is typically gold or silver, so if you see a gold or silver band, it's safe to assume this is the tolerance band.

HOW TO WRITE LARGE VALUES

Our resistance color chart shows some resistance values written with *k* and *M* in front of the Ω symbol. These are part of a shorthand that makes it easier to write really large values. If you have a resistor that's 300,000 Ω, it's common to shorten that to 300 kΩ instead, where *k* is short for *kilo*, which means one thousand. The *M* stands for *mega*, which means one million. So instead of writing 3,000,000 Ω, you could write 3 MΩ.

What Are Resistors Made Of?

To create a resistor, you could just use a really long piece of standard wire. Wires have a bit of resistance, and the longer your wire is, the more resistance you'll get. But using miles of wire to reduce current isn't very efficient. It's better to use a material that has more resistance, such as carbon. Often the resistors that you buy in stores are made of carbon wrapped inside an insulating material.

Resistors Control Current and Voltage

At first, you might find the resistor a bit boring. If you connect one to a battery, you probably won't see anything happen; the resistor might just get warm, and you might wonder what the big deal is. On the other hand, if you use a resistor with a very low resistance value, such as 10 Ω, then it could get *really* hot—hot enough to give you a burn—and the battery might die pretty quickly.

WARNING   *Connecting a low-value resistor directly between positive and negative points can be dangerous on some types of batteries. Some batteries are strong enough to make your resistor burst into flames. Be careful!*

But the cool thing about resistors is that you can use them to change the voltages and currents in your circuit! That means that you get to be the master of your circuit and decide how it should behave.

INTRODUCING OHM'S LAW

The key to controlling the current and voltage in your circuit is a formula called *Ohm's law*. Ohm's law relates resistance, voltage, and current as follows:

$$V = I \times R$$

Here's what those letters mean:

V   Voltage, measured in volts (V)

I   Current, measured in amps (A)

R   Resistance, measured in ohms (Ω)

Given these definitions, in English, Ohm's law reads, "Voltage equals current multiplied by resistance." You can also write the Ohm's law formula in the two following forms:

$$R = \frac{V}{I} \qquad\qquad I = \frac{V}{R}$$

Let's put Ohm's law to work. Imagine you have a resistor and a 9 V battery, and you want 0.05 A of current to flow in the resistor. How much resistance do you need in the resistor to get the right amount of current flowing? Use Ohm's law to find out:

$$R = \frac{V}{I}$$

$$R = \frac{9 \text{ V}}{0.05 \text{ A}}$$

$$R = 180 \ \Omega$$

180 Ω

9V

After dividing the voltage by the current, you'll find that to get 0.05 A of current flowing in the resistor, you need a 180 Ω resistor.

PROJECT #7: LET'S DESTROY AN LED!

Almost all electronics have some LEDs, which I introduced in Chapter 3. Where there are LEDs, there are also resistors. Look around a house, and there's a big chance you'll see a few. For example, check a computer, a washing machine, a television, or a Wi-Fi router. Do you see some blinking lights when you push buttons? Those are very likely LEDs in series with resistors.

In "Project #6: Turn On a Light with Lemon Power" on page 58, you just connected an LED to your homemade lemon battery, and that was it. In most circuits, however, you need to take a bit more care to make sure you don't break your LED. If too much current flows through an LED, it becomes really hot and burns out. The lemon battery was too weak to provide enough current to break the LED.

Of course, I could tell you all this forever, but trying things in real life is the best way to learn! I had to break a few LEDs myself before I accepted that I couldn't connect them directly to a battery without a resistor, and I want you to see what that's like, too. That's why in this project, you're going to destroy an LED!

Shopping List

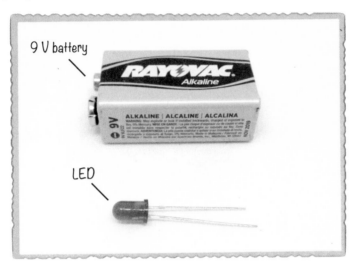

▸ **A standard LED** (Jameco #333973, Bitsbox #OP002).

▸ **A standard 9 V battery** to power the circuit.

Step 1: Identify Which LED Leg Is Which

Look at your LED closely, and you should see that one leg is longer than the other. LEDs are *polarized*, which means that current flows through them only if you connect them a certain way in your circuit. The longer leg is called the *anode*; it's the leg that you connect to the positive side of the battery. The shorter leg is called the *cathode*, and you connect it to the negative side of the battery.

On some LEDs, the legs are the same length. In that case, find the flat side on the bottom of the LED itself. The leg on the flat side is the cathode.

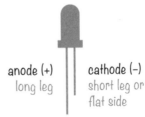

anode (+)
long leg

cathode (−)
short leg or
flat side

Step 2: Break That LED!

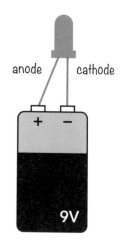

anode   cathode

To avoid burning your fingers, hold your LED by one of the legs. Then, place the 9 V battery on the table and touch the legs of the LED directly to the battery terminals.

The LED should glow brightly for a short moment, become hot, and then go dark. Parts of it may actually turn black. Congratulations: You just broke your first LED!

NOTE *Some LEDs stop working after a second when connected directly to a battery. Others may give a bit of light for a few seconds.*

Step 3: What If Nothing Happens to the LED?

If nothing happens, there are three likely causes:

▸ You connected the LED backward.

▸ Your LED is already broken.

▸ Your battery is dead.

First, try connecting your LED to the battery the other way around. If you're sure it's connected the right way, then either your LED is already broken or your battery is dead. Try replacing the battery first; if that doesn't work, replace the LED. Now, you should be able to break your LED.

HOW TO USE AN LED CORRECTLY

Even though it's pretty fun to destroy LEDs, it's better to know how to *avoid* destroying an LED. Your LED burned because it had too much current running through it, but you can prevent that with your trusted friend the resistor. Resistors resist the flow of current, and if you choose the right resistance value, they'll resist the current enough to get just the right amount of current for your LED.

HOW TO WRITE SMALL VALUES

In electronics projects, you often need to deal with very small values, especially when measuring or calculating current. For example, most current values in the circuits in this book are less than 0.1 A, and many are closer to 0.02 A. To simplify writing these values, I typically use the prefix *milli*, which is written as a lowercase *m*. It means one thousandth, so 1 mA is 0.001 A. Because 1,000 mA is the same as 1 A, 0.02 A becomes 20 mA, and 0.1 A becomes 100 mA.

Protecting Your LED with a Resistor

An LED in a circuit should always have a resistor in series with it. Of course, resistors come in many different values, and to figure out the right one for your circuit, you need to do a little math.

Most standard LEDs need a voltage of about 2 V and a current of about 20 mA, or 0.02 A, to light up. These two values, together with the voltage of your battery, are all you need to figure out the correct resistance. Just put these two values into the following formula:

$$R = \frac{V_{\text{BAT}} - V_{\text{LED}}}{I_{\text{LED}}}$$

If this formula looks familiar, that's because it's actually just another version of Ohm's law. The two *V*s and the *I* are still voltage and current, but V_{BAT} is the battery voltage, V_{LED} is the voltage your LED needs to light up (often 2 V), and I_{LED} is the current your LED needs (often 20 mA). You'd read this formula as "To find the resistance, subtract the LED voltage from the battery voltage and divide the result by the LED current."

Calculating the Resistance You Need

Imagine you have a 9 V battery, a resistor, and a standard LED. What resistance value should the resistor be? Using the formula from the previous section, you should get:

❶ $R = \dfrac{V_{\text{BAT}} - V_{\text{LED}}}{I_{\text{LED}}}$

❸ $R = \dfrac{7\text{ V}}{0.02\text{ A}}$

❷ $R = \dfrac{9\text{ V} - 2\text{ V}}{20\text{ mA}}$

❹ $R = 350\ \Omega$

That means you need a resistor of 350 Ω to get the right amount of current flowing through the circuit.

PROJECT #8: POWERING AN LED

Now let's power a standard LED with a protective resistor so the LED doesn't burn out. We just calculated that to power an LED with a 9 V battery, you need a resistor of 350 Ω.

But as I explained in "Resistor Color Codes" on page 70, standard resistor values aren't always exactly the resistance you need. If you buy a 350 Ω resistor, it isn't necessarily 350 Ω, but maybe 370 Ω. And not all resistance values are even available. For a resistor in an LED circuit, having the exact value isn't important. That's fortunate because you won't find any 350 Ω resistors in standard resistor packs. Instead, you can use a 330 Ω resistor, which is a standard value that's easier to find.

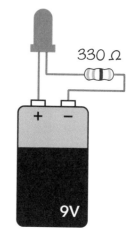

330 Ω

9V

Shopping List

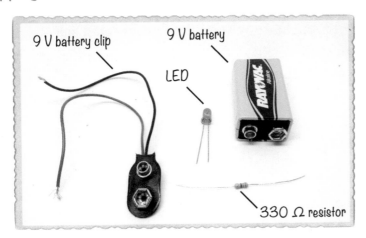

- ▶ **A standard 9 V battery** to power the circuit.
- ▶ **A 9 V battery clip** (Jameco #11280, Bitsbox #BAT033) to connect the battery to the circuit.
- ▶ **A standard LED** (Jameco #333973, Bitsbox #OP002)
- ▶ **A 330 Ω resistor** (Jameco #661386, Bitsbox #CR25330R for just this value or Jameco #2217511, Bitsbox #K017 for a variety pack) for limiting the current to the LED.

Step 1: Twist the Resistor and LED

First, connect the short leg, or the cathode, of the LED to one side of the resistor. It doesn't matter which side of the resistor you connect; just twist the resistor leg around the LED leg.

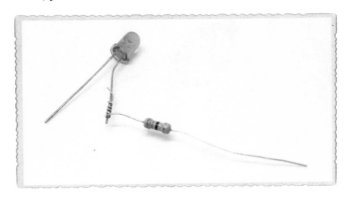

Step 2: Wire the Battery Clip

Twist the battery clip's red wire onto the long leg of the LED. Then twist the black wire to the unconnected side of the resistor.

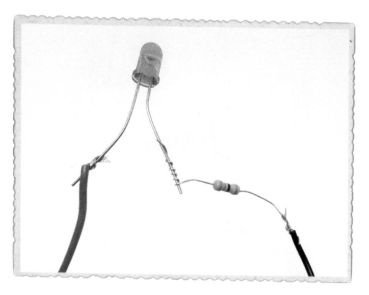

Step 3: Let There Be Light!

Now, plug your battery into the clip, and your LED should glow!

Step 4: What If the LED Doesn't Work?

If your LED doesn't turn on, first disconnect the battery and make sure you've connected the components exactly as I described in Steps 1 through 3. Having someone else review your wiring can be helpful, too; ask a parent, sibling, or friend to look it over.

If your connections look right and the LED is still dark, then double-check the LED's orientation; just about anyone who's ever built an electronics project has connected an LED backward at least once. The long leg is the anode, and in this project, it should connect to the positive side of the battery.

BUILDING CIRCUITS ON A BREADBOARD

Up to now, you've connected circuits with tape or by twisting component legs together, but this isn't very practical when a circuit has more than a few components. Fortunately, a *breadboard* can make connecting components easier. Breadboards have holes that you can stick component leads into to create circuits. When you're done, you can just unplug all the components and reuse them in different projects!

How to Connect Components and Wires

Inside a breadboard, metal plates connect the holes you see on the outside in a certain pattern. Let's look at a breadboard with four connection areas—two supply areas and two component areas.

In the supply areas on both sides, all the holes in each *column* are connected. You'll typically plug the positive side of your circuit's *power supply*—like the batteries you've used so far—into the red columns, and you'll typically plug the negative side of the power supply into the blue columns. Throughout this book, I'll refer to the supply column marked with a red line as the *positive supply column*, and I'll refer to the supply column marked with a blue line as the *negative supply column*.

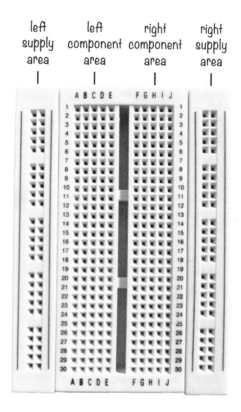

In the component areas, all the holes in each *row* are connected, and the columns are not connected. The left and right component areas are separated so that there's no connection between them. For example, holes A, B, C, D, and E in row 1 are connected, and holes F, G, H, I, and J in row 1 are connected, but holes E and F in row 1 are not connected.

To plug a component into a breadboard, simply push it into the hole where you want the connection. For example, if you wanted to connect one side of a resistor to the positive side of an LED, you'd just insert both the leg from the resistor and the leg from the LED into two holes on the same row in the left or right component area. If you have two component legs or wires that shouldn't connect, just make sure they are either on different rows in the component area or on opposite sides of the component area.

Wires to Use on a Breadboard

Eventually, you want to connect one row on your breadboard with a different row. You can use a wire to make that connection, but not all wires work well on a breadboard. The wire has to be stiff enough that you can push it into the hole without it bending, and it has to be thick enough to fit all the way inside the breadboard hole without falling out. *Single-strand* wires are the best wires for building circuits on a breadboard because they have one solid core inside, instead of many tiny wires wrapped together. The thickness of wire you need depends on your breadboard, but wires with 0.016- to 0.028-inch diameters should work. Wire thickness is often given in *American wire gauge (AWG)*, and I recommend using wire that is 21 to 26 AWG. You can buy wires that are cut and stripped for simple use with breadboards, or you can cut and strip your own wires using a wire cutter.

Another option is to use breadboard *jumper wires*. These wires have stiff ends that are very easy to connect to a breadboard. If you plan to connect a lot of circuits on a breadboard (you should!), keep a bunch of breadboard jumper wires on hand to make your life easier.

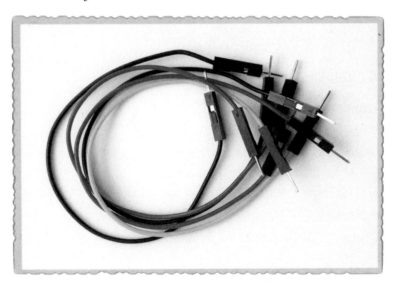

PROJECT #9: YOUR FIRST BREADBOARD CIRCUIT

Let's connect a simple circuit on a breadboard! Just as in "Project #8: Powering an LED" on page 78, this circuit lights up an LED, but this time we'll build the circuit on a breadboard. In this project, we're not going to use the supply rails on the side because the circuit is so simple that it makes more sense just to connect it all on the component area.

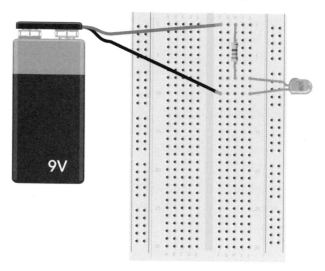

Shopping List

▶ **A breadboard** (Jameco #20601, Bitsbox #CN329) with at least 30 rows.

▶ **A standard 9 V battery** to power the circuit.

▶ **A 9 V battery clip** (Jameco #11280, Bitsbox #BAT033) to connect the battery to the circuit.

▶ **A standard LED** (Jameco #34761, Bitsbox #OP003).

▶ **A 330 Ω resistor** (Jameco #661386, Bitsbox #CR25330R for just this value or Jameco #2217511, Bitsbox #K017 for a variety pack) for limiting the current to the LED.

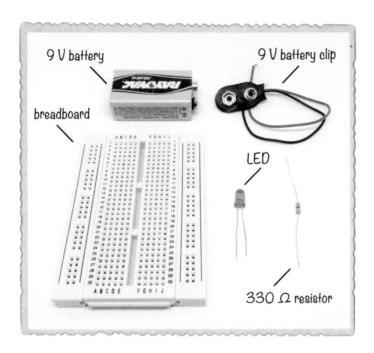

9 V battery

9 V battery clip

breadboard

LED

330 Ω resistor

Step 1: Place the Resistor

First, place one leg of the resistor in row 1 and the other in row 8.

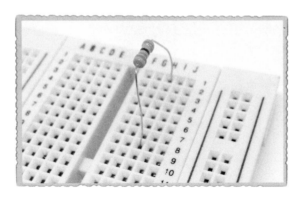

Step 2: Place the LED

Remember, LEDs are polarized, and they must be connected the right way to work. Connect the long leg of the LED to row 8, where the resistor leg is connected. Because the resistor and LED legs are on the same row, they're now connected. Connect the other leg of the LED to row 10.

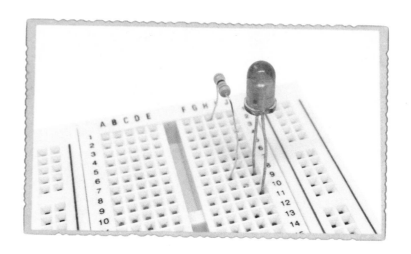

Step 3: Place the Battery Clip

Now, connect the battery to the LED and resistor. Connect the battery clip with the red wire at row 1 and the black wire at row 10. Plug your battery into the clip, and your LED should light up!

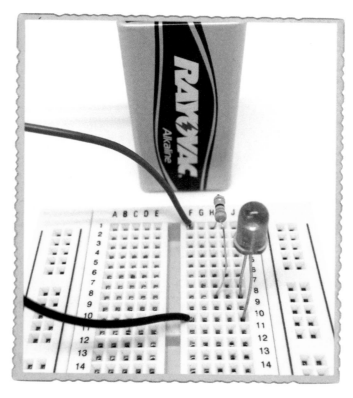

Step 4: What If the LED Doesn't Work?

If your LED doesn't glow, first disconnect the battery. You should always disconnect the battery when making changes to your circuit. Then, check whether the short leg of the LED is connected to the negative side of the battery.

If your LED is still not working once it's oriented correctly, check that your components are connected exactly as described in Steps 1 through 3. Are the long leg of the LED and one of your resistor's legs in row 8? Is the positive battery lead in the same row as the other resistor leg? Is the negative battery lead in row 10 with the short LED leg? Ask someone else to have a look at your circuit, too; maybe they can help you find the problem.

WHAT'S NEXT?

In this chapter, you've learned about two very common components: the resistor and the LED. You also learned how to use Ohm's law to calculate resistance, current, and voltage values. This knowledge will form the foundation for many aspects of electronics that you'll explore throughout this book.

You also learned to use a breadboard, which is a useful skill. To practice placing circuits on a breadboard, try building one of the projects you did earlier in this book without tape! How would you re-create "Project #2: Intruder Alarm" on page 11 on a breadboard?

In the next chapter, you'll learn about two more components: the capacitor and the relay. Then, I'll show you how to build one of my favorite circuits—a circuit that blinks a light!

5

BLINKING A LIGHT FOR THE FIRST TIME

W hen I was a kid, one of my very first electronics projects was making a light blink. It was amazing to see the circuit work for the first time, and now I want to share that experience with you. In this chapter, you'll learn how the capacitor and the relay work. These are two common and very interesting electronics components, and I'll show you how to have some fun with them. At the end, you'll build your very own blinking light!

MEET THE CAPACITOR

The *capacitor* is like a rechargeable battery; you can charge a capacitor and use its energy to power something. But a battery can hold much more energy than a capacitor. A battery can power an LED for days without recharging, while most capacitors can power one for only a few seconds at most.

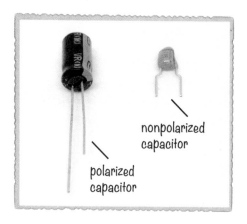

Capacitors are often used to introduce time delays in a circuit. For example, because a capacitor stores energy, it could be used to keep an LED on for a bit more time, even after the power is shut off. This little trick can be used with other components, too, to create interesting results.

How Capacitors Work

On the inside, capacitors are very simple devices. They're made of two metal plates placed very close together, with a material such as paper in between. To save space, the metal plates and the material between them are folded or rolled into a compact package.

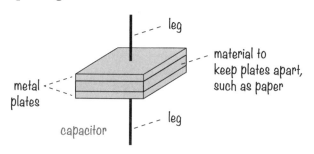

When you connect a battery to the two sides of a capacitor, a current flows as the battery tries to push electrons through the capacitor. But electrons can't flow across the gap between the plates, so instead, electrons build up on one plate and leave the other plate. Eventually, one plate can't hold anymore electrons, and the current stops flowing; at that point, we say that the capacitor is *fully charged*.

But just like the electrons in a battery, the electrons in the capacitor don't like being crowded together on the one plate. They want to go over to the side with fewer electrons. This means you have stored potential energy in your capacitor. If you disconnect the battery and connect, for example, a resistor between both sides of the capacitor, the stored electrons on one plate will start flowing the other way around, through the resistor, in order to reach the plate with few electrons.

Polarized and Nonpolarized Capacitors

Capacitors can be either *polarized* or *nonpolarized*. Like an LED, a polarized capacitor has a positive and a negative leg, and its positive leg must always face the positive terminal of the battery. The black capacitor shown in the photo is polarized, and its negative leg is marked with a stripe and minus signs down the side. The yellow capacitor isn't polarized, so it doesn't matter which leg goes where.

WARNING *Take care when you use polarized capacitors for the projects in this book and in your own projects. You must connect them the correct way to prevent them from being damaged.*

In all circuits that call for a capacitor, you can use a nonpolarized capacitor as long as you can find one with the right *capacitance*. Capacitance is measured in farads (F), and the more capacitance a capacitor has, the more energy it can store. Nonpolarized capacitors with large capacitances aren't made because they'd have to be physically very large. Polarized capacitors are able to hold more energy in a smaller space, but they have the disadvantage of needing to be connected the correct way around.

When building circuits with high capacitance values, you'll be using polarized capacitors. Always make sure the positive leg of any polarized capacitor is connected closest to the positive side of the battery.

Capacitor Values

The capacitors you'll use in this book will have capacitances in the μF (microfarad), nF (nanofarad), or pF (picofarad) range. Capacitances tend to be very small, and they're often written with the *micro*, *nano*, and *pico* prefixes, which are defined as follows:

▶   μ (micro) means *millionth*, so 1,000,000 μF = 1F

▶   n (nano) means *billionth*, so 1,000,000,000 nF = 1F

▶   p (pico) means *trillionth*, so 1,000,000,000,000 pF = 1F

Polarized capacitors are big enough to have their values written on them. Nonpolarized capacitors, on the other hand, are a bit trickier. They're usually really small, so they tend to have cryptic codes like *104* or *202*. I always forget what they mean, so when I need to figure out what a certain code means, I just look it up in a table. You can find a table of common codes in "Capacitor Codes" on page 283.

But like most things, capacitors are much more interesting to play with than to read about. Build the next project, and you'll see for yourself how a capacitor works.

PROJECT #10: TEST A CAPACITOR

This project demonstrates that a capacitor stores energy. It's nearly the same circuit you built in "Project #9: Your First Breadboard Circuit" on page 84, but this time, you're going to add a capacitor. When you remove the battery from the circuit, as shown here, you'll see that the LED remains lit for a second or two. That's because the capacitor is powering the LED using its stored energy.

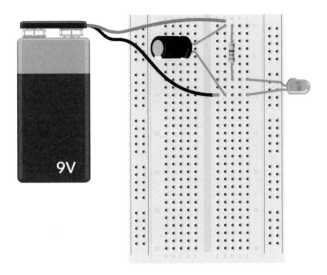

Shopping List

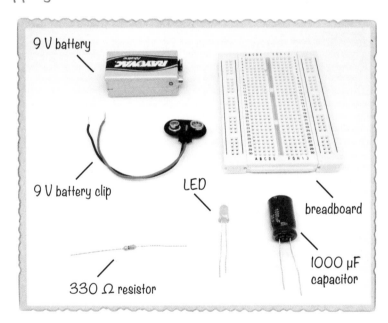

9 V battery

9 V battery clip

LED

breadboard

330 Ω resistor

1000 µF capacitor

▶ **A breadboard** (Jameco #20601, Bitsbox #CN329) with at least 30 rows.

▶ **A standard 9 V battery** to power the circuit.

▶ **A 9 V battery clip** (Jameco #11280, Bitsbox #BAT033) to connect the battery to the circuit.

- **A standard LED** (Jameco #34761, Bitsbox #OP003)
- **A 330 Ω resistor** (Jameco #661386, Bitsbox #CR25330R) for limiting the current to the LED.
- **A polarized 1000 µF capacitor** (Jameco #158298, Bitsbox #EC1KU25)

Step 1: Start with the LED Circuit

Follow the instructions from "Project #9: Your First Breadboard Circuit" on page 84, making sure you end up with a working circuit that lights an LED. Then, disconnect the battery and move on to the next step.

Step 2: Add the Capacitor

Connect your capacitor to the battery. Because the capacitor is polarized, place the pin marked with a minus sign or a zero in the same breadboard row as the battery's negative leg. Connect the other leg to the same row as the battery's positive leg, as shown.

Step 3: Charge the Capacitor

Connect the battery to the clip, and the LED should light up. At the same time, the battery should have very quickly charged the capacitor.

Step 4: Use the Capacitor to Light the LED

Watch the LED while removing the battery. The LED shouldn't turn off right away when you disconnect the battery. Instead, it should stay lit for a second or so and then fade out slowly until there's no more energy left in the capacitor.

Step 5: What If the Circuit Doesn't Work?

First, check whether the circuit works without the capacitor. If not, then go back to Step 1 and get the LED circuit working before you move forward.

If the LED lights up with the battery connected but turns off the instant you remove the battery, then something is wrong with the capacitor part of your circuit. Check that the capacitor's positive leg is connected to the positive battery leg (row 1 in the photo) and that the other leg is connected to the negative battery leg (row 10 in the photo).

If the circuit looks correct, confirm that the capacitor value is at least 1000 µF; the value should be written on the capacitor. If it's less than 1000 µF, try a bigger capacitor.

DESCRIBING CIRCUITS WITH SYMBOLS

So far, you've built circuits with only a few components. To build more interesting electronics projects, you usually need more components. But drawing out every component in a big circuit exactly as it looks in real life can be messy and time-consuming. This is where *circuit diagrams*, also called *schematics*, come to the rescue.

In a circuit diagram, each component has its own simple symbol, which lets you draw the whole circuit quickly. As with words and books, until you know what the different symbols mean, a circuit diagram might look a bit complex. Let's jump right in and learn a few symbols! Here's a circuit with an LED, a resistor, and a battery, alongside its circuit diagram:

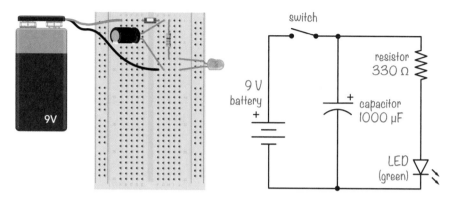

The battery symbol has a + sign to tell you where the positive leg goes. Sometimes you'll see the battery symbol without the plus sign; in that case, the positive side is the one with the longest line.

NOTE *The battery symbol may be drawn with two lines, with four lines, and sometimes with even more lines. Regardless of the number of lines, just look for the specified voltage and use a battery with the same voltage.*

The switch symbol is very simple, and it doesn't matter which way you draw it. In the LED symbol, the line on the point of the triangle indicates the negative side of the LED, or the cathode. Check that against the "real-life" version, and you can see that the LED's positive leg is indeed connected to the resistor in both diagrams. The resistor, on the other hand, isn't polarized, so its symbol doesn't have any directional markers. There are both polarized and nonpolarized capacitor symbols, but our example shows the polarized version, which has the positive side marked with a + sign. Look at both the circuit and the circuit diagram again—do you agree that they are the same?

Once you learn how to build something just by looking at a circuit diagram, a whole new world will open up for you. You can find circuit diagrams for almost anything on the Internet these days, like radios, MP3 players, walkie-talkies, or whatever you want to build! I'll teach you more circuit symbols throughout this book as we use more components.

MEET THE RELAY

I was a very curious child, and I always wondered how things worked. To me, electronics devices like the radio or the television were just magical. I had no idea how they worked, and I didn't believe I'd ever understand how to make one.

But one day, I asked my dad how it was possible to blink a light automatically. I thought that if I could only understand that, I'd be able to understand more. Fortunately, my dad was an engineer, and he was also good at explaining things in a practical way. When I asked him how to blink a light, he introduced me to a *relay*, like the one shown here.

relay

Chapter 1 described how you can use switches to turn things on and off. Chapter 2 showed you how to use an electromagnet to move things. Imagine combining the electromagnet with a switch: instead of pushing a button to change the switch's position, you add an electromagnet that can change the switch position for you. That's the idea behind the relay, and this illustration shows how it works:

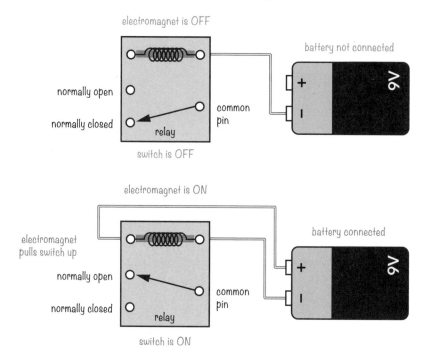

The white dots represent the relay's pins. Notice that the connections are labeled *common pin*, *normally closed*, and *normally open*. These labels are defined as follows:

Common pin (COM)   Connected to either NC or NO

Normally closed (NC)   Connected to COM when coil is off

Normally open (NO)   Connected to COM when coil is on

When the battery isn't connected to the relay coil, the electromagnet doesn't pull, and COM from the switch is connected to NC. But when you connect the battery to the relay coil, the electromagnet turns on, and the switch is pulled so that COM gets connected to NO instead. You can connect or disconnect a battery from the electromagnet to change the position of the switch!

Using the Relay to Blink a Light

If you were to connect a relay to a battery so that the electromagnet connects to the battery through the relay's COM and NC switch contacts, the electromagnet would turn on and off continuously. Here's an example relay circuit that's also connected to a light bulb:

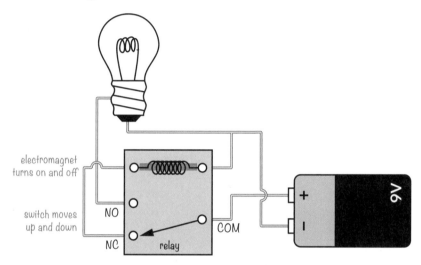

Before you connect the battery in this circuit, the electromagnet would be off, leaving the COM and NC switch contacts connected. With the battery connected to the circuit, the electromagnet would receive power from the battery through the switch. This means it'd pull the switch and connect COM and NO instead, giving the light bulb power from the battery.

But with the switch in this position, the battery would no longer be connected to the coil, and the electromagnet would lose its power. When the electromagnet has no power, the switch falls back to its original position, disconnecting the battery from the light bulb. The battery would power the electromagnet again, and the process I just described would repeat.

In this example, it seems like you'd get a blinking light, right? In theory, yes. But the relay would switch on and off so fast you wouldn't see the light turn on and off properly! Instead, you'd hear a really fast ticking sound as the relay switched back and forth, but the light would appear to stay dark.

Slowing Down the Blinking

To build a circuit that lets you actually see the light blink, you need to slow down the relay. The capacitor can help with this. In "Project #10: Test a Capacitor" on page 92, adding a capacitor to the LED circuit made the LED stay on for a short time after the battery was disconnected. If you connected a capacitor across the electromagnet in our too-fast blinking-light circuit, the electromagnet would stay on for a bit, too.

But the electromagnet wouldn't stay off for long, so in this case, the light would appear to be on all the time. To make it stay off longer, you'd need to slow down the charging of the capacitor so it wouldn't jump back to fully charged as soon as it discharged. To do this, you could reduce the amount of current flowing into the capacitor. And how do you reduce the amount of current? With a resistor! To blink an LED light with a relay, you'd use a circuit like this one, which we're going to build next:

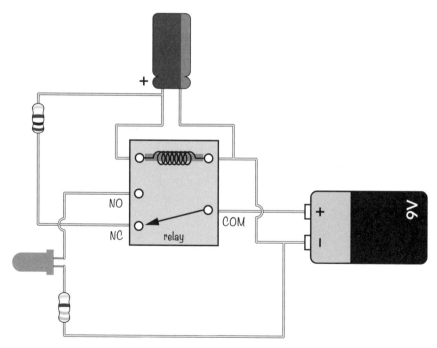

PROJECT #11: BLINK A LIGHT!

It's time for you to build your first blinking light by flashing an LED. Here's the complete circuit diagram—do you recognize the components?

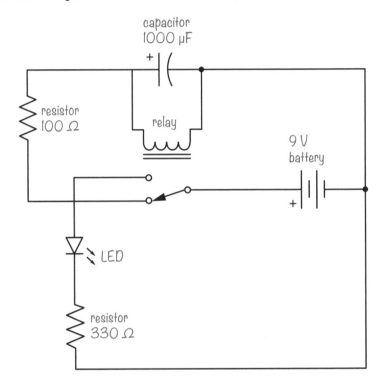

When connecting a circuit, it's helpful to connect it in a way that looks like the circuit diagram. That makes it easier to find out what's wrong if your circuit isn't working later—and you'll often find that your circuit doesn't work on the first try. Tracking down errors and figuring out how to fix them is part of the game!

Shopping List

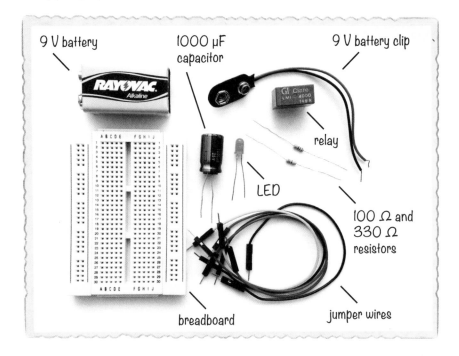

- ▶ **A breadboard** (Jameco #20601, Bitsbox #CN329) with at least 30 rows.
- ▶ **Breadboard jumper wires** (Jameco #2237044, Bitsbox #CN236) for making easy connections. (Standard hookup wire works, too.)
- ▶ **A standard 9 V battery** to power the circuit.
- ▶ **A 9 V battery clip** (Jameco #11280, Bitsbox #BAT033) to connect the battery to the circuit.
- ▶ **A DPDT or SPDT relay** (Jameco #842996, Bitsbox #SW073) with a 5 V, 6 V, or 9 V coil.
- ▶ **A standard LED** (Jameco #34761, Bitsbox #OP003)
- ▶ **A polarized 1000 µF capacitor** (Jameco #158298, Bitsbox #EC1KU25)

- ▶ **A 100 Ω resistor** (Jameco #690620, Bitsbox #CR25100R) for limiting the current to the capacitor.
- ▶ **A 330 Ω resistor** (Jameco #661386, Bitsbox #CR25330R) for limiting the current to the LED.

Step I: Identify the Relay Pins

Not knowing which pin on the relay is which is the biggest source of error when building this circuit, so let's look at these pins now. To find the function of each pin, look up the *datasheet* for your relay. A datasheet is a document that tells you how an electrical component works. For a relay, it should say what voltage you need for the electromagnet coil, how much current you can run through the contacts, and so on. You should be able to find a link to the datasheet on the product page where you bought your relay.

For the relay I recommend, the pins are placed as shown here:

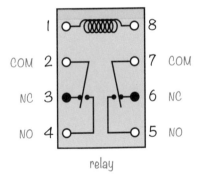

relay

This type of diagram is called a *pinout*, and it shows the function of each pin. The view is from above with the pins out of sight below the plastic case of the relay. I suggest drawing the pinout on a piece of paper and keeping it on your desk while you connect the circuit so you can check it repeatedly and make sure you're connecting it the right way.

In this relay, pins 1 and 8 are for the electromagnet coil—you can identify these pins by the line at the top. When you look at the real relay with the line at the top, the pins should be in the same places as in the pinout.

The pinout also shows that there are two switches inside. Pins 2 to 4 make up one switch, and pins 5 to 7 make up the other. Don't worry about memorizing the relay pins, though. You can always refer to the pinout if you get stuck, and I encourage you to do so whenever you need to. Also, different relay types can have different pinouts.

Step 2: Make the Relay Switch Fast

First, let's connect the relay so that it switches on and off automatically. Place the relay in the middle of your breadboard, centered over the notch, with one side in each component area. This way, no pin should be connected to any other pins.

Plug your battery clip's positive leg into the positive supply column on the left, and plug the negative leg into the negative supply column on the same side. Connect a jumper wire from the negative supply column to the same row as the right coil pin (pin 8), shown as row 9 this diagram:

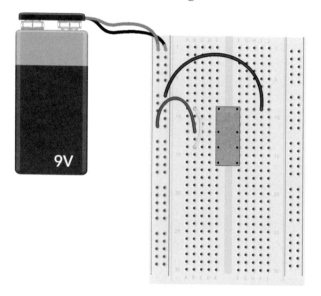

Next, connect a wire from the plus column on the left to the relay's common switch pin (pin 2). In this diagram, the common pin is in row 12, column B. Then, connect a wire from pin 3 on the relay (the NC pin) to the coil pin (pin 1); this is the yellow wire going from row 14 to row 9 in column B in the diagram. Connect the 9 V battery, and you should hear a really fast ticking. This is the relay turning on and off. Disconnect the battery for now.

Step 3: Make the Relay Stay On Longer

The next step is to slow down the relay by placing a capacitor across the coil of the electromagnet. Connect the capacitor as shown here:

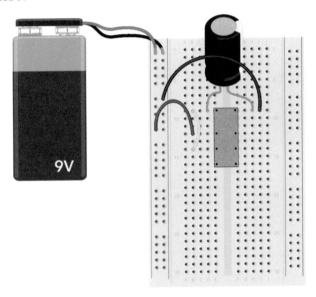

In the diagram, I've connected the negative capacitor leg to pin 8 on the relay by plugging it into row 9, column H and connecting the positive leg to pin 1 on the relay at row 9, column D. Whichever holes you use, just make sure you connect the capacitor's negative leg to the same relay pin as the one you connected the negative supply to. The negative capacitor leg is usually marked with a stripe, a zero, or a minus sign.

Connect the battery to test your circuit. You'll know it's working if you hear the telltale ticking sound. The ticking should be much slower now, which means that the relay is staying on for a longer time. But in the instant the relay is turned off, the capacitor should charge again, leaving the relay off for only a fraction of a second. You'll fix that in the next step, so disconnect the battery again now.

Step 4: Make the Relay Stay Off Longer

Let's add a resistor before the capacitor to reduce the amount of current that flows and force the capacitor to take more time to charge. To do this, simply replace the wire between pins 1 and 3 on the relay (the yellow wire connected to rows 9 and 14 in my diagrams) with a resistor of about 100 Ω as shown here:

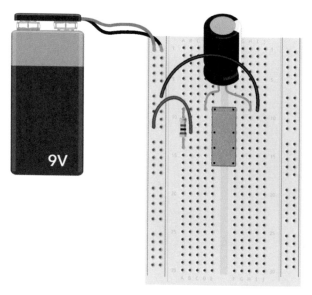

Connect the battery to test it. The relay should stay off a bit longer now, and you'll recognize this by the "tick-tock" sound of the relay.

Step 5: Add the LED and Resistor

Disconnect the battery and add the LED and the 330 Ω resistor to the circuit. Connect the long leg of the LED to the NO pin of the relay (pin 4). My LED's long leg is connected to row 16, because the NO pin is plugged into that row. Connect the other leg to an unconnected row below, such as row 19. Connect the resistor from the same row to the negative column on the supply side.

Your breadboard should look something like this:

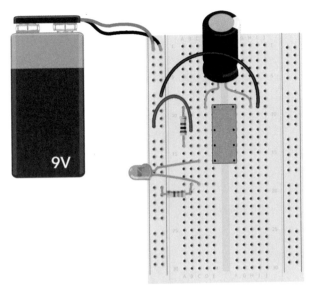

Compare this to the circuit diagram at the beginning of the project to see how the symbols match. Now, connect the battery and watch the light blink!

Step 6: What If the LED Won't Blink?

If you can't get the LED to blink, go back to Step 1 and check your work through to Step 4. This should give you a relay that turns on and off automatically. If that works, then you should be able to connect the LED and resistor to have a working circuit.

If the LED still doesn't blink, confirm you've connected it according to the diagrams. Still no luck? Remove the LED and the resistor from the circuit, and then connect only these two to the battery until you can make the LED light up. (Follow the instructions in "Project #9: Your First Breadboard Circuit" on page 84.) If you can't make the LED light, then your LED may be broken or your resistor may be the wrong value.

TRY IT OUT: MAKE YOUR INTRUDER ALARM MORE EFFECTIVE

Try connecting a relay to the Intruder Alarm you built in Project #2 on page 11 so that when someone tries to enter a room, they can't turn off the alarm by closing the door. When your relay is triggered by a switch, it should stay on. This diagram shows how you can connect the relay (shown in blue) to the rest of the circuit (shown in black). When the alarm is triggered, the beep will continue to sound until you disconnect the battery.

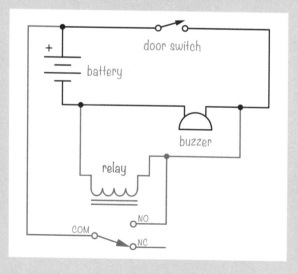

WHAT'S NEXT?

You've come a long way in this chapter! So far, you've learned how four common components in electronics work (resistors, LEDs, capacitors, and relays), you've connected a few circuits on a breadboard, and you've even made your own project that blinks a light. Hopefully, you understand why the light blinks, too.

You've already connected a few circuits on a breadboard, which is a useful skill when you want to test a circuit or build simple prototypes. But when you want a circuit's components to stick together forever, you need to solder them, and I'll show you how in the next chapter.

6

LET'S SOLDER!

n Chapter 5, you used a breadboard to build new circuits. A breadboard lets you quickly test new ideas and experiment with different components to see the result, but it isn't a permanent solution. Components can easily fall out, and there can be loose wires all over the breadboard. When you want to use a circuit for a long time without changing it, it's better to solder the circuit to a *circuit board*. Soldering is kind of like gluing: you melt a material called *solder* onto the component legs so the components stick to the circuit board. A circuit board has holes like a breadboard, and when you solder components to it, they become connected by plates of copper.

This chapter will teach you how to solder, starting with a simple LED circuit. This will give you the foundation you need to solder your own circuits later. After you've practiced the basics in this chapter, you'll continue soldering in Chapter 7 to build a touch-enabled switch and a circuit that wakes you up when the sun rises in the morning.

HOW TO SOLDER

To solder a circuit, you need a few tools:

▶ Solder

▶ A soldering iron

▶ A stand to hold the soldering iron

▶ A damp sponge

▶ Safety goggles

Solder is a mix of metals that can easily melt at high temperatures. The most commonly used solder melts at around 360 to 370 degrees Fahrenheit.

A *soldering iron* is a pen-shaped tool that heats up to a temperature high enough to melt solder. If you put solder on the tip of the soldering iron, the solder melts.

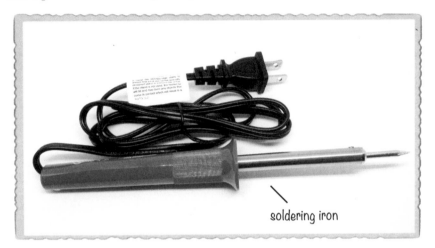

soldering iron

Soldering is quite easy once you learn the basics, and one important basic step is to take a few safety precautions.

Soldering Safety Tips

Soldering irons get extremely hot, and you can burn yourself if you touch the metal part of a soldering iron while it's plugged in. Always return the soldering iron to its stand when you're not using it; never lay it directly on a surface. Avoid touching *joints* (soldered connections) and components for a few seconds after you solder them, too. They can get hot enough to burn.

Here are some other important safety tips to keep in mind while soldering:

▶ Keep the hot parts of the soldering iron away from the power cord.

▶ If you're soldering on a table, protect the surface with a piece of wood or some thick cardboard.

▶ Always wash your hands after handling solder.

▶ If you do get burned, don't panic. For a minor burn, immediately cool the burn with running cold water, keeping the burned area under water for at least five minutes. Putting ice on a burn is good, too, but make sure to do the initial cooling with water right away.

Ask an adult to supervise your first few attempts at soldering, and remember: soldering is fun, but soldering irons must still be used with great care. With those tips in mind, read the rest of this section for a step-by-step guide to basic soldering.

Heat the Soldering Iron

The first step of soldering is to plug in your soldering iron and place it on your stand. Don't forget to put on your safety goggles!

After a minute or two, check whether the iron is hot enough by touching some solder to the tip of the iron. If the solder melts, your iron is ready to go.

Clean the Soldering Iron Tip

Touch the tip of your soldering iron to a damp sponge to clean it. A clean tip transfers heat much better than a dirty one, so clean the tip often.

Tin the Soldering Iron Tip

Here's a little trick: to heat the joint faster, add a bit of solder to the tip of the soldering iron just before you start soldering. This is called *tinning*. This must be done just a second or two before soldering to be effective.

Heat Both the Pin and the Pad

Place the tip of the soldering iron onto both the component leg and the copper strip. Heat the strip and leg for a couple of seconds before you move on to the next step.

Add Solder

While keeping the soldering iron tip on the joint, touch some solder to the leg and the copper strip. As the solder melts, slowly add more until there's just enough to coat both the leg you're soldering and the copper strip you want to connect it to. When you have enough melted solder, remove the solder wire from the joint while still keeping the soldering iron tip on the joint.

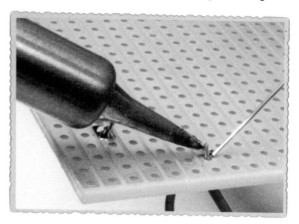

Remove the Soldering Iron

Finally, remove the soldering iron tip from the joint and place the iron in its stand. Always do this last. If you remove the iron while the solder wire is touching the solder joint, the solder wire may get stuck to the circuit board when the solder joint hardens.

Your solder joint should have a cone shape.

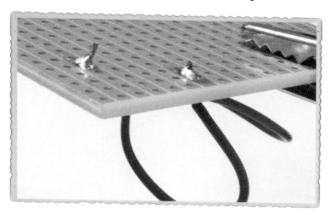

If you're done soldering, then unplug the iron so it can cool down.

Watch Out for Bad Solder Joints!

It's important to heat both the component leg and the copper strip with the iron before touching solder to either. When you heat only the component leg and not the copper strip, the solder sticks to the leg, but there's no connection between the solder and the copper strip. If only the strip is heated, the solder will stick to the strip, but not the leg. It could look like a good soldering joint from a distance, but the solder probably won't be connected to the leg.

You must also make sure the solder doesn't float over to another copper strip next to it. This will create an unintended connection between the two strips.

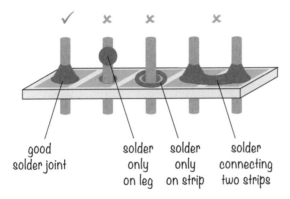

good
solder joint

solder
only
on leg

solder
only
on strip

solder
connecting
two strips

If your solder joint doesn't look right, don't worry. Just reheat the joint, the component leg, and the copper strip and add more solder to achieve the cone shape of a good solder joint. Then, you should be good to go.

PROJECT #12: SOLDER YOUR FIRST LED CIRCUIT

Now, let's get soldering! In this project, you'll solder the resistor and LED circuit from "Project #8: Powering an LED" on page 78 to a circuit board. The battery should make current flow in the circuit, the resistor should make sure there isn't too much current, and the LED should light up.

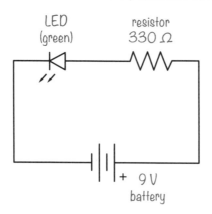

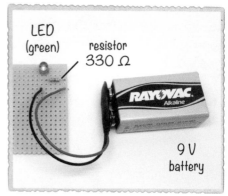

Shopping List

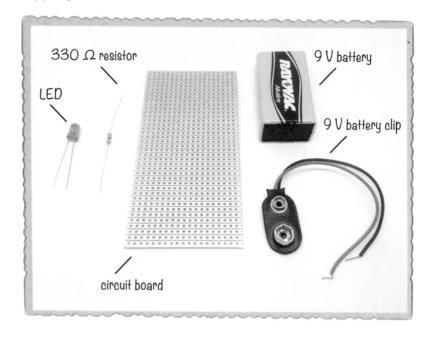

- **A standard 9 V battery** to power the circuit.
- **A 9 V battery clip** (Jameco #11280, Bitsbox #BAT033) to connect the battery to the circuit.
- **A circuit board** (Jameco #2191488, Bitsbox #HW005) with copper strips.
- **A standard LED** (Jameco #34761, Bitsbox #OP003)
- **A 330 Ω resistor** (Jameco #661386, Bitsbox #CR25330R) for limiting the current to the LED.

Tools

- **A soldering iron** (for example, Jameco #116572, Bitsbox #TL031)
- **A stand** (for example, Jameco #36329, Bitsbox #TL032) to hold the soldering iron.
- **A roll of standard solder wire** (for example, Jameco #94570, Bitsbox #HW022)

▶ **A wet sponge** to clean the tip of the soldering iron.

▶ **A wire cutter** (Jameco #35482, Bitsbox #TL008) to cut off excess legs from components.

Step 1: Place the Components

Look at your circuit board and get familiar with the connection pattern on it. The circuit board I recommend is called a *prototyping board*, and it's covered with little straight strips of copper, each with lots of holes. Any component leads that you solder into holes that share a strip of copper will become electrically connected.

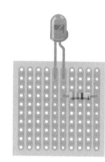

Place your resistor and LED legs through the circuit board. The resistor should share a copper strip with the LED's positive lead. Note that the strips shown in the figure are on the bottom side of the board, which is why they're not copper colored in the picture. Anytime a project involves soldering to a circuit board, I'll show shadows of the copper strips so you can see where the connections are underneath.

Step 2: Bend the Component Legs

Carefully flip your circuit board over so you can see the copper; hold the LED and resistor in place with a finger if needed so they don't fall out. Then, slightly bend each component's legs outward so that the LED and resistor stay in place even with the copper side up. Keep the board copper-side-up for now.

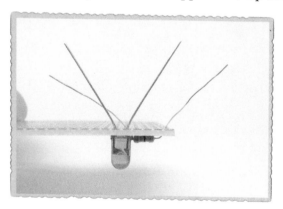

HOW TO READ THE CIRCUIT BOARD ILLUSTRATIONS

Throughout this book, you'll see circuit board illustrations I created in a program called Fritzing. These illustrations show the top side of the circuit board so you can see how the components look, and they show the bottom side—a slightly darker color than the top—so you can see how the copper strips look.

When following my instructions, always orient your circuit board with the copper strips on the bottom going in the same direction shown in the illustration. If you ever get confused about how you should read the connections in a circuit board illustration, just refer back to this example.

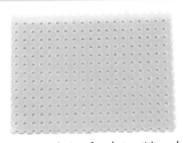

top view photo of real circuit board

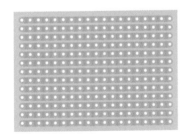

top view illustration showing copper
strip locations underneath

If you want to create your own circuit illustrations with Fritzing, you can download the free, open source software from *http://www.fritzing.org/*.

Step 3: Heat and Clean the Soldering Iron

Your components should be in place and ready to solder, so plug in and heat up the iron now. This may take a few minutes. As always, check to see whether the iron is hot enough by touching some solder to the tip to see whether it melts.

Before you start soldering, clean the tip of the soldering iron, too. Wet your sponge just a little bit and wring out any excess water. Then, wipe the tip of the iron on the sponge to remove any old solder.

Step 4: Solder the Resistor and LED

With the copper side of the circuit board facing up, solder each component leg to the board, as described in "How to Solder" on page 112. Your board should look like this:

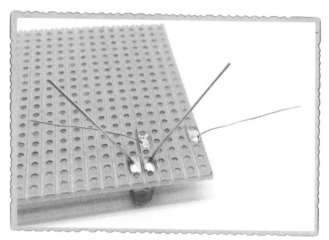

Step 5: Trim the Legs

Right now, your LED and resistor have really long legs. You don't want to leave them sticking out because stray metal can create unintentional paths between components. At best, that could prevent your circuit from working until you move the leg away from the component it shouldn't be touching; at worst, an unintended connection could break a component. To prevent accidental connections, cut off each leg just above the solder joint. The legs could go flying when you cut them, so turn the board away from your eyes or wear safety goggles for protection.

TIP *Hold the circuit board over an empty box while you cut the legs off, to prevent the scraps from getting lost and to make cleanup easier. You could also rest the circuit board on a table and hold the leg with one hand while you clip.*

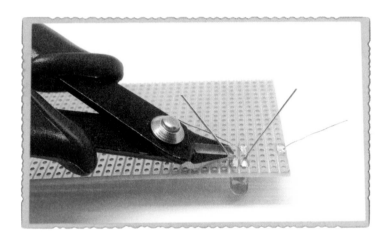

Step 6: Solder the Battery Clip

This circuit also needs a way to connect the battery to the components, so solder the battery clip to the circuit board now.

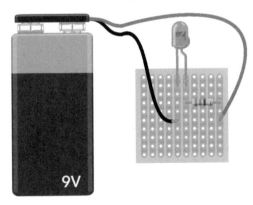

The red wire from the battery clip is the positive wire; connect it to the copper strip that connects only to the resistor, not the LED. The black wire is the negative lead, so connect it to the negative side of the LED. Your circuit board should now look like this:

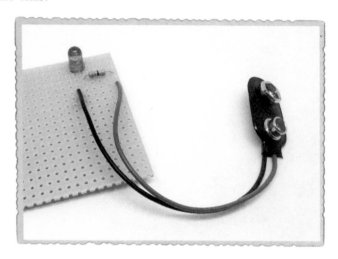

Step 7: Let There Be Light!

Now, let's test your circuit. Plug in the battery, and your LED should light up!

Step 8: What If the Soldered LED Circuit Doesn't Work?

If your LED doesn't light, check that you don't have any unintentional connections. Is solder connecting two joints that shouldn't connect? Are extra long component legs making contact?

Next, inspect your solder joints closely. Do any of them look like the examples of bad connections described in "Watch Out for Bad Solder Joints!" on page 117? If so, you might need to flow a little more solder: warm up your iron again and try to make sure your solder joints look like little pyramids.

Check the placement of the LED, too. Did you connect it correctly? Because you've cut off the excess legs, you can't see which leg is longer anymore, but if you look closely at the LED, you should see that one side of the base of the plastic housing is flattened. This is the negative side, which should be connected to the battery clip's black wire. If you've placed it the wrong way, here's one quick fix: use your wire cutters to cut the battery clip leads, removing the clip from the circuit board. Now, solder the positive battery lead where the negative lead used to be, and solder the negative battery lead where the positive lead used to be. This works because it doesn't matter which side of the LED the resistor is on.

OOPS! HOW DO I REMOVE A SOLDERED COMPONENT?

Sometimes, you'll make mistakes when soldering. For example, what if you soldered the battery clip the wrong way or used a 33,000 Ω resistor instead of a 330 Ω one? Well, don't worry: even the most experienced engineers mess up at soldering sometimes, and there's a way to fix your circuit when it happens. In these cases, you need to *desolder*, which just means to remove the solder from a solder joint.

Solder wick is a very useful tool for desoldering, and I suggest keeping some at your side any time you solder. The solder wick is made of braids of copper thread, so it's also called *desoldering braid*.

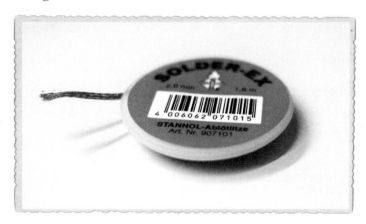

When you place a piece of solder wick on top of a solder joint and heat both together, the solder should melt as usual, and the solder wick should absorb the liquid solder just as a dry cloth absorbs water. When you remove the solder wick, the solder should be on the wick instead of on the circuit board!

PROJECT #13: DESOLDER THE BATTERY CLIP

Knowing how to desolder is very useful, and not just for fixing soldering mistakes. For example, desoldering will let you exchange a broken component in a circuit for a fresh one—or you can desolder a component to reuse it in another circuit. In this project, I'll show you how to desolder your battery clip from the previous project.

Shopping List

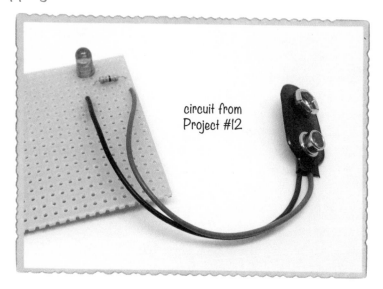

circuit from
Project #12

▶ **The circuit from "Project #12: Solder Your First LED Circuit" on page 118**

Tools

▶ **A soldering iron** (for example, Jameco #116572, Bitsbox #TL031)

▶ **A stand** (for example, Jameco #36329, Bitsbox #TL032) to hold the soldering iron.

▶ **A wire cutter** (Jameco #35482, Bitsbox #TL008) to cut the solder wick.

▶ **Solder wick** (Jameco #153462, Bitsbox #HW082) to remove the solder.

soldering iron

stand

solder wick

wire cutter

Step 1: Heat the Soldering Iron

Plug in your soldering iron and wait for it to heat. To test the temperature, touch some solder wire to the tip; the solder will melt when the iron is warm enough.

Step 2: Place the Solder Wick on the Solder Joint

Lay the end of your solder wick on top of the solder joint for one battery clip wire.

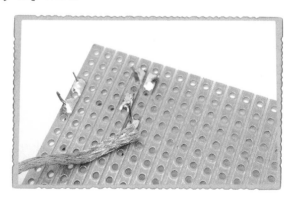

WARNING *Solder wick can get very hot when you heat it with the soldering iron, so don't hold the metal part by your fingers.*

Step 3: Heat the Solder Joint and the Solder Wick

Place the tip of the heated soldering iron on top of the solder wick, directly over the solder joint you want to desolder.

After a few seconds, the solder should melt and flow onto the braid. Lift the braid from the board, together with the soldering iron.

Step 4: Trim the Used Solder Wick

Remove the braid from the joint and look at it. The braid should have solder in it.

Much like a dirty cloth, this bit of wick is too dirty to use anymore. Use your wire cutter to cut off the piece that has solder inside.

Now, inspect your solder joint. If there's no solder left connecting the component leg to the circuit board, then you should be able to remove the wire from the hole. If not, repeat Steps 2 and 3 with a fresh bit of solder wick, and then repeat Step 3 until you can remove the wire.

Step 5: Remove the Other Battery Clip Wire

Repeat Steps 2 to 4 for the other battery clip wire, and you should be able to completely remove the battery clip from the circuit board. At this point, the copper side of your circuit board should look something like this:

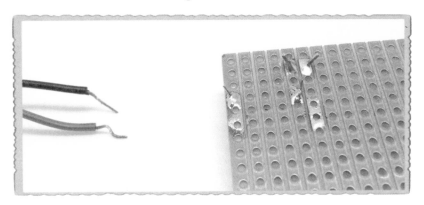

TRY IT OUT: SOLDER MORE STUFF!

Are you itching to get some extra soldering practice? One fun way to practice is to buy and build electronics *kits*, which include components and a circuit board that you can solder. You can also find circuit diagrams online, buy the necessary components, and solder them on a prototyping board, just as you did in this chapter.

Here are some online stores that sell both kits and components:

▶ **Jameco:** *www.jameco.com*
▶ **Adafruit:** *www.adafruit.com*
▶ **SparkFun:** *www.sparkfun.com*

WHAT'S NEXT?

In this chapter, you learned a very useful skill: soldering. This means you can make permanent circuits for your projects without worrying that they'll fall apart. And with a little practice at desoldering, you can take projects apart on purpose, too.

In Chapter 7, I'll introduce you to the transistor, the photoresistor, and the potentiometer. These are some really exciting components that you can use to make your circuit come alive and respond to its surroundings. For example, I'll show you how to create a circuit that tells you when the sun rises in the morning!

7

CONTROLLING THINGS WITH ELECTRICITY

Electronic components let you build smart things, like a lamp that turns on when it gets dark or a door that opens automatically when you approach it. In this chapter, you'll learn about a new component that will help you build such smart objects: the transistor.

The previous chapter showed you how to solder, and this chapter's projects—a touch sensor and an alarm that wakes you up when the sun rises—will give you more chances to practice your soldering skills. All you need for each project is the transistor and a few additional components.

MEET THE TRANSISTOR

The *transistor* is the most important component in electronics, and if you've ever heard experienced hardware enthusiasts talk about it, you've probably noticed that they tend to use a lot of difficult words. But the transistor really isn't hard to understand; in fact, you've already used something that acts a lot like one! Do you remember the relay you learned about in Chapter 5? The transistor is similar to the relay in many ways: it's like a switch that you can open and close with electricity.

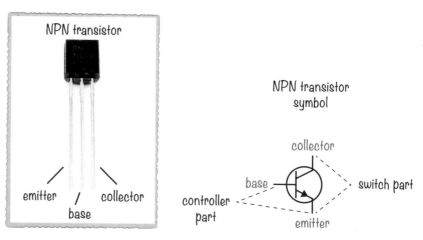

A transistor has three legs. In a standard *NPN transistor*, the three legs are called *emitter*, *base*, and *collector*. You'll often see these labeled *e*, *b*, and *c* in circuit diagrams. You turn the transistor on and off—that is, you open and close the switch—with the base and emitter legs, and you connect a circuit that you want to control between the collector and the emitter legs.

When you look at our example transistor with the flat side facing you, the leftmost leg is the emitter, the middle leg is the base, and the rightmost leg is the collector. But this is not the case for all transistors, so always check the datasheet for your transistor to find out which leg is which.

Why Use a Transistor?

If a transistor acts like a switch, then you might be wondering when you'd want to use a transistor instead of a switch in the first place. Well, think about a fan: if it's hot in your room and you want to turn a fan on, you have to manually flip a switch. But if that fan were part of the right kind of circuit with a transistor and a few other components, you could make the fan turn on automatically when the temperature in your room rises above 75 degrees Fahrenheit. To make this happen, you'd need one circuit that could sense temperature and another circuit that could turn on a fan.

Now, imagine a temperature-sensing circuit that gives a voltage when the temperature is above 75 degrees and no voltage if the temperature is below. If you were to connect one wire from the fan to an NPN transistor's collector, connect the fan's other wire to the positive terminal of the battery, and connect the transistor's emitter to the battery's negative terminal, the transistor would control when the fan is switched on.

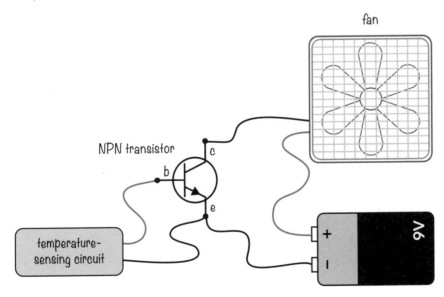

Then, you could connect the output of the temperature-sensing circuit to the controlling part of the transistor—that is, the base and emitter. In such a circuit, the fan would turn on when the temperature rises above 75 degrees and turn off when the temperature is less. Let's look at how the transistor's "switch" closes in the first place.

How the Transistor Works

When a little bit of current flows from the base of a transistor to the emitter, the transistor "closes the switch" so that current can also flow from the collector to the emitter.

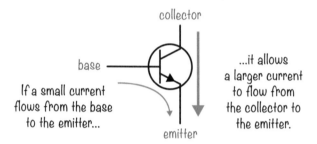

In Chapter 1, I explained that voltage pushes current through a circuit. For current to flow from the base to the emitter, there needs to be a voltage to push that current. When the current flows from the base to the emitter, this opens a path for the current to flow between the collector and the emitter. You can also control the amount of current that flows between the collector and the emitter by changing the current flowing from the base to the emitter.

The specific type of transistor we're talking about is an *NPN-type bipolar junction transistor*. This long name describes the materials inside the transistor. There's some advanced chemistry and physics behind how it works, but you don't need to know all of that to build cool circuits with a transistor—you just need to know what the transistor does.

The important thing to remember for now is that different transistor types exist. For each transistor project in this book, just use the type I describe in the Shopping List sections, and your circuits will work just fine. And of course, when you build circuits outside this book, be sure to use the type of transistor specified in the circuit diagram.

Controlling an LED with a Transistor

Other projects in this book have used this simple LED circuit, complete with a resistor and a battery:

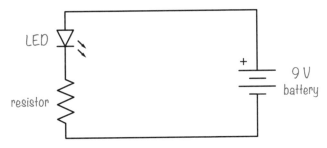

Based on what you've learned so far, what do you think would happen if you put a transistor between the resistor and the battery's negative terminal?

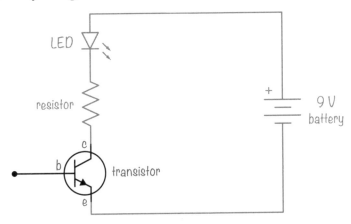

With no voltage on the transistor's base, or the controlling pin, no current flows from the base to the emitter. That means no current can flow between the collector and the emitter either, and the LED would be off.

But if you were to apply a small voltage to the base—for example, by connecting a small battery to it—the transistor would let current flow from the collector to the emitter, and the LED would glow. A transistor that allows current to pass is considered *on*; a transistor that doesn't allow current to pass is considered *off*. The amount of voltage needed to turn an NPN transistor on is about 0.7 V, so a circuit like this one would allow current to pass through properly to light the LED:

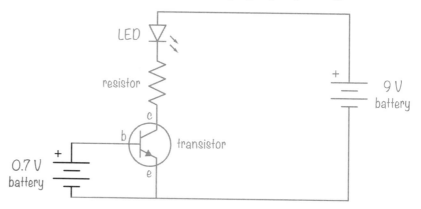

Normally, you wouldn't connect a battery to the base. Instead, you'd connect another circuit that you want to control the transistor, like a light-sensing circuit that gives a small voltage when it detects light. A circuit like that would turn the transistor on and off according to the light.

You can build a circuit like this to control LEDs and other components. In the next project, I'll show you how to use a transistor to turn an LED on with the touch of your finger.

PROJECT #14: BUILD A CIRCUIT THAT SENSES TOUCH

Did you know that your finger can act as a resistor? Your finger has a resistance of a few megohms (MΩ), and that's a lot! This resistance varies, though. If your finger is sweaty, for example, the resistance decreases.

In this project, you'll use your finger as a resistor to complete a circuit that turns on an LED, creating a touch sensor. A *sensor* is a component that can measure things in the world around you, like light or temperature. In many cases, a sensor is a resistor that changes its value based on light level, temperature, or some other physical quantity you might want to know about.

If you connect a resistor of a few megohms between the positive side of your battery and the base of the transistor in this circuit, a small current should flow through the base of the transistor to the emitter. This current should be large enough to turn the transistor on and let a little bit of current flow from collector to emitter.

This circuit has a transistor, a resistor, an LED, and a battery, just like the one in the previous section. This time, instead of a separate battery, you'll connect the 9 V battery to the transistor's base with your finger through a kind of touch pad. The touch pad will just be two exposed wires placed close enough together that you can touch both with your finger at the same time.

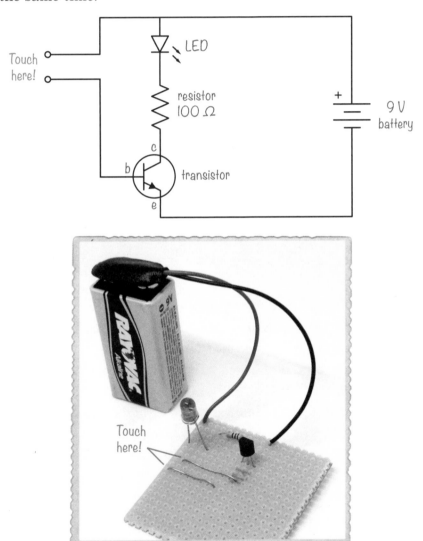

Notice that instead of a 330 Ω resistor with the LED that you used before, this circuit uses a 100 Ω resistor. Often the resistance in your finger is so high that the transistor won't turn on fully. With a smaller resistor, you should still get a bright LED, even if your finger's resistance is a bit high.

Shopping List

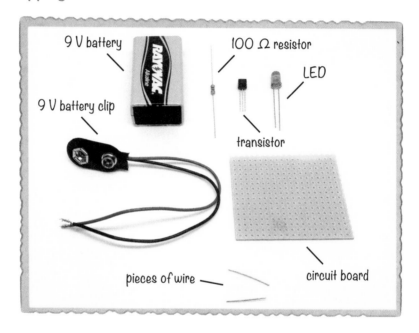

- ▸ **A standard 9 V battery** to power the circuit.
- ▸ **A 9 V battery clip** (Jameco #11280, Bitsbox #BAT033) to connect the battery to the circuit.
- ▸ **A circuit board** (Jameco #2191488, Bitsbox #HW005) with copper strips.
- ▸ **A standard LED** (Jameco #34761, Bitsbox #OP003)
- ▸ **Two pieces of exposed wire**, each about 1 inch long. You could also use two legs you cut from components in other projects.
- ▸ **A transistor 2N3904** (Jameco #38359, Bitsbox #QD018)
- ▸ **A 100 Ω resistor** (Jameco #690620, Bitsbox #CR25100R) for limiting the current to the LED.

Tools

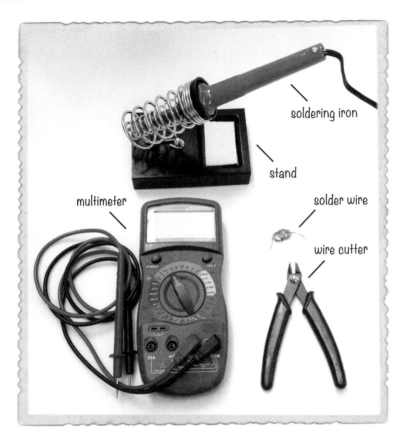

- **A soldering iron** (for example, Jameco #116572, Bitsbox #TL031)
- **A stand** (for example, Jameco #36329, Bitsbox #TL032) to hold the soldering iron.
- **Solder wire** (for example, Jameco #94570, Bitsbox #HW022)
- **A multimeter** (Jameco #2206061, Bitsbox #TL057, Rapid Electronics #55-6662) to measure voltages if the circuit doesn't work.
- **A wire cutter** (Jameco #35482, Bitsbox #TL008) to cut off excess legs.

Step 1: Place Components on the Prototyping Board

Place the LED, the resistor, and the transistor into the proto-typing board as shown. Make sure a copper strip connects the resistor to (1) the LED's cathode leg and (2) the transistor's collector leg. Bend the legs on the copper side of the board so that the components stay in place.

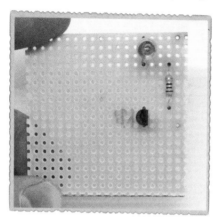
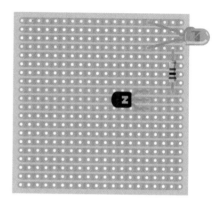

Step 2: Check Your Component Placement

Before soldering, look on the copper side of the board and double-check that your components are placed according to the directions in Step 1. Inspect the orientation of the LED and the transistor specifically, as these must be soldered the correct way for your circuit to work.

Step 3: Solder the Components and Trim Excess Legs

Solder the components to the board, just as you learned in "How to Solder" on page 112, and then use your wire cutters to cut off the excess legs. Wear your safety goggles and take care to turn the board away from yourself in case bits of wire fly off as you cut.

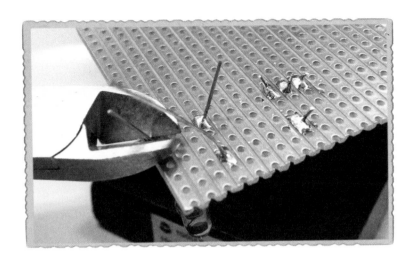

Step 4: Solder the Touch Pad

Next, solder the two pieces of exposed wire. Connect one wire to the LED's anode leg, with the other end on an empty copper strip. Connect the other wire to the base of the transistor, also with the other end on an empty copper strip. Solder them in such a way that you can touch both with your finger.

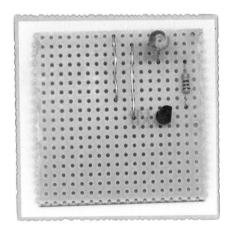

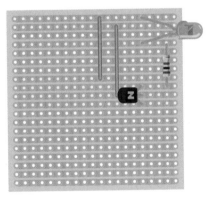

Step 5: Power It Up!

Now you need power! To finish the job, first solder the battery clip to the board, placing the red and black wires as shown at ❶. After you've soldered the battery clip, plug the battery into it at ❷.

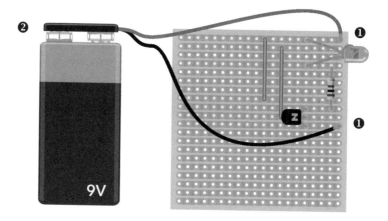

This touch-sensor circuit is ready to test!

Step 6: Test the Sensor

Touch both exposed wires at the same time with your finger. Your LED should light up. If you can't see the LED glow, try turning out the light in your room; the LED might just be dim. If you still can't see the LED glowing, dip your finger in water and try again, as wetting your finger reduces its resistance.

WARNING   *Use only a finger to touch the exposed wires. If you use something with a very low resistance, like a piece of wire, you can destroy the transistor.*

Step 7: What If the Touch Sensor Doesn't Work?

If nothing happens when you touch the wires, start by checking the direction of your LED and your transistor. It's very common to mix up the pins of these components, so go back to Step 1 and make sure they're connected on the prototyping board's copper strips, according to the images.

If the LED and the transistor are connected correctly, you can use your multimeter to measure the voltage between the base and the emitter of the transistor on the controller side, without touching the touch pad. Set your multimeter to a DC voltage range—20 V DC, for example—and then connect one multimeter cable to the base leg and one to the emitter leg, as shown. The multimeter should show a value around 0 V. Now, place your finger on the touch pad and measure the voltage again. The multimeter should show around 0.7 V.

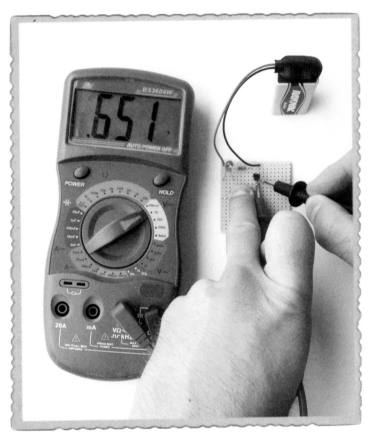

If the controller side of the transistor is fine, check the switch side. Measure the voltage from one leg of the LED to the other, without touching the touch pad. You should see 0 V on the multimeter. Place your finger on the touch pad and measure again; now it should be around 1.7 to 2 V.

If either multimeter measurement gives you incorrect values, then check your connections against the circuit diagram one more time, paying extra attention to the two exposed wires. Finally, check your solder joints, look for stray pieces of wire or solder bridging the gap between copper strips, and fix any bad connections you find.

> ### TRY IT OUT: CAN THE TOUCH SENSOR DETECT DIFFERENT TOUCHES?
>
> Try touching the two exposed wires lightly and note the brightness of the LED. Now, try pressing really hard. Can you see any difference? Have a friend repeat the experiment. Was the LED's brightness when your friend touched the wires different from when you touched them? If so, that means your friend's finger has a different resistance!
>
> When you press harder, the connection between the wires and your finger improves, reducing the resistance so it's easier for the current to flow.
>
> Here's another fun thing to try with a friend: Touch one of the wires yourself and have your friend touch the other. Then, hold your friend's free hand with your free hand. Can you see the LED light up? Now, the current goes from the battery through both of your bodies and into the transistor. But don't worry—the current is so low that it's not dangerous and you won't feel anything.

RESISTORS THAT CAN CHANGE VALUE

Up until now, you've used only resistors that have a fixed resistance, but you can also find resistors that have a *variable* resistance value, which means the resistance can change. For example, some resistors change value when you turn a knob, while others change their value based on the temperature or the amount of light. This section introduces two variable resistors: the potentiometer and the photoresistor.

Meet the Potentiometer

In Chapter 4, you learned about the standard resistor, a component that has a certain, unchangeable resistance. The *potentiometer* is also a resistor, but it has a variable resistance, and it's often used to control things such as the volume of a speaker. (You know the volume control on the radio? That's often a potentiometer.) A potentiometer usually has three pins and a shaft you can rotate to change the resistance.

potentiometer

potentiometer symbol

The potentiometer symbol represents how the potentiometer works and the functions of the three pins. The resistance between pins 1 and 3 is a fixed resistance of a certain value. This value is equal to the value listed when you buy the potentiometer. If you have a 10 kΩ potentiometer, for example, then the resistance between pins 1 and 3 will be 10 kΩ.

Pin 2 is called the *wiper*. It connects to the resistor somewhere between pins 1 and 3. You can change the position of the wiper by turning the shaft of the potentiometer. If you turn the shaft so that the wiper comes closer to pin 1, the resistance between pin 1 and the wiper gets smaller, but the resistance between pin 3 and the wiper becomes larger.

Meet the Photoresistor

A *photoresistor* is another variable resistor. *Photo* means *light*, and this component's resistance changes with the amount of light shining on the top of it. Sometimes this component is also called a *light-dependent resistor (LDR)* because its value depends on light.

Photoresistors are made of a material with some special properties. In the dark, this material has a high resistance, but when light shines on it, the light energizes electrons that would otherwise be bound in the material. Those energized electrons can flow freely through the material, reducing the resistance. The more light that shines on the photoresistor, the less resistance it has.

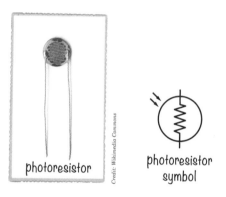

photoresistor

Credit: Wikimedia Commons

photoresistor symbol

DIVIDING A VOLTAGE WITH RESISTORS

When the resistance of a photoresistor or potentiometer in a circuit changes, the voltage and/or the current must change, too, according to Ohm's law. (See "Introducing Ohm's Law" on page 73 if you want to walk through the math again.) If you make your variable resistor part of a circuit called a *voltage divider*, you'll get a voltage output that varies with the resistance. You can use that changing voltage to control another component in your circuit. Knowing how to identify voltage dividers can also help you understand how other circuits work.

What Does a Voltage Divider Look Like?

If you connect two resistors with the same resistance to each other and to the positive and negative sides of a battery, the voltage where your resistors meet will be half the battery voltage—for example, 4.5 V if you use a 9 V battery. This circuit is called a *voltage divider*.

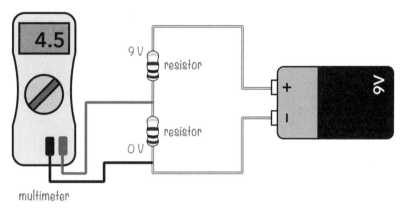

If you use unequal resistors instead of identical ones, you can use a voltage divider to get voltages anywhere from 0 V up to your battery voltage. You just need to do a little bit of math.

Calculating the Voltage from a Voltage Divider

Let's say you have the following circuit. What's the output voltage (V_{out}) from this circuit?

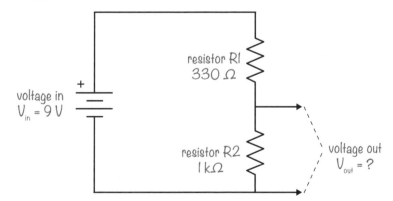

To find V_{out}, enter the values from the circuit into the following formula:

$$V_{out} = V_{in} \times \frac{R2}{R1 + R2}$$

$$V_{out} = 9\text{ V} \times \frac{1000\ \Omega}{330\ \Omega + 1000\ \Omega}$$

$$V_{out} = 9\text{ V} \times 0.752$$

$$V_{out} = 6.77\text{ V}$$

In this example, the output voltage is 6.77 V—roughly two-thirds of the 9 V input from the battery.

How a Voltage Divider Can Help Measure Light

In the beginning of this section, I mentioned that the voltage divider can help you measure light, but how do you do that? Just replace one resistor in the voltage divider with a photoresistor, and you'll get a circuit that outputs a voltage based on the amount of light shining on it. And by adjusting the other resistor in the voltage divider, you can set the circuit to give a certain voltage at a certain light level. Connect the output of this circuit to a transistor that controls a buzzer, and you've got yourself a light-controlled alarm!

PROJECT #15: BUILD A SUNRISE WAKE-UP ALARM

It's time to combine all the concepts you've learned in this chapter into one fun project: a sunrise wake-up alarm!

This circuit starts an alarm when it detects light. After you build it, you can place it in your window (between any curtains and the glass) when you go to bed. When the sun rises, your circuit should detect the light and start the alarm, leaving you with no choice but to get up and turn it off.

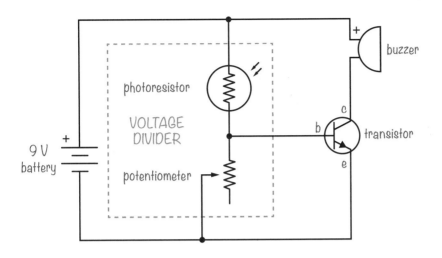

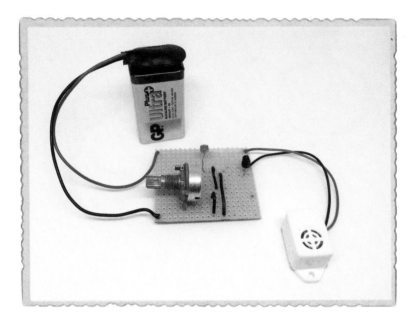

This project uses a transistor, a photoresistor, a potentiometer, and a buzzer. The photoresistor and the potentiometer create the voltage divider, and the output of the voltage divider is connected to the base of the transistor. The amount of light the photoresistor detects will determine whether the transistor is on or off. If the transistor is on, current should flow through the buzzer, and the buzzer should make sound. The potentiometer is there to set how much light the circuit needs before the alarm triggers.

Shopping List

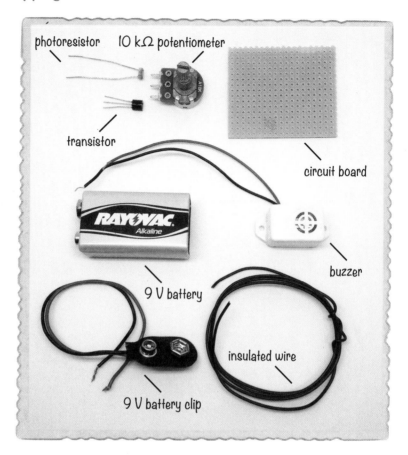

- ▸ **A standard 9 V battery** to power the circuit.
- ▸ **A 9 V battery clip** (Jameco #11280, Bitsbox #BAT033) to connect the battery to the circuit.
- ▸ **A circuit board** (Jameco #2191488, Bitsbox #HW005) with copper strips.
- ▸ **Insulated wire** (Jameco #36792, Bitsbox #W106BK), about 10 inches in length. Standard hookup wire works fine.
- ▸ **A transistor 2N3904** (Jameco #38359, Bitsbox #QD018)
- ▸ **A 10 kΩ potentiometer** (Jameco #2118791, Bitsbox #VR004)

- **A photoresistor** (Jameco #202454, Bitsbox #ST004) for detecting light.
- **A buzzer** (Jameco #2173870, Bitsbox #ST016) that beeps. Buzzers come in both active and passive versions. You'll need an active buzzer that works with 9 V in this project, just like the one you used in "Project #2: Intruder Alarm" on page 11.

Tools

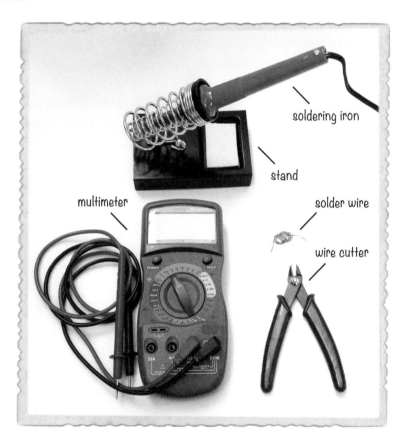

- **A soldering iron** (for example, Jameco #116572, Bitsbox #TL031)
- **A stand** (for example, Jameco #36329, Bitsbox #TL032) to hold the soldering iron.
- **Solder wire** (for example, Jameco #94570, Bitsbox #HW022)

- ▶ **A multimeter** (Jameco #2206061, Bitsbox #TL057, Rapid Electronics #55-6662) to measure voltages if the circuit doesn't work.
- ▶ **A wire cutter** (Jameco #35482, Bitsbox #TL008) to cut off excess legs.

Step 1: Place Components on the Prototyping Board

Start by placing the transistor, the photoresistor, and the potentiometer on the board, as shown. Bend the legs of the photoresistor and transistor on the other side so that they stay in place. The top copper strip will be the positive battery connection, and the bottom copper strip will be the negative one.

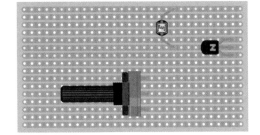

The diagram shows the components and the copper tracks underneath, while the photo shows what your board should look like in real life.

Step 2: Solder the Components and Trim the Legs

Check the placement of the components closely against the circuit diagram at the beginning of the project and the illustration in Step 1. Make sure the transistor is connected the right way and that the photoresistor has one leg on the same copper row as the center pin of the transistor. Each of the other pins, including each pin on the potentiometer, should be on a row of its own.

When you're sure your components are placed correctly, solder the pins to the board.

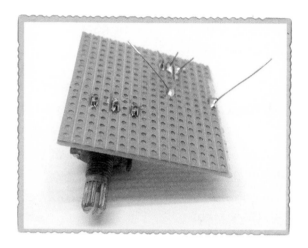

When you're finished soldering, cut off the excess legs.

Step 3: Add the Buzzer to the Board

Next, solder the buzzer to the board. Place the buzzer's positive (red) lead through a hole in the top copper row together with the photoresistor. Then place its negative (black) lead in the same row as the collector leg of the transistor. Solder both now.

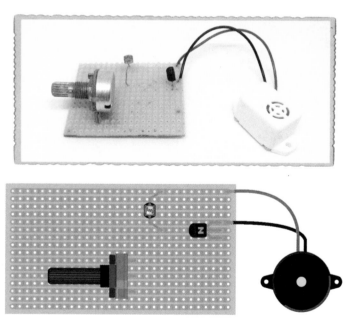

Step 4: Make the Remaining Connections with Wires

If you compare your circuit to the circuit diagram, you'll see that you're still lacking a few connections to make the circuit complete. The circuit board is missing the battery clip, but to work when powered, the circuit also needs the following connections:

▶ The base of the transistor needs to connect to the upper potentiometer pin.

▶ The middle potentiometer pin needs to connect to the negative battery terminal.

▶ The emitter of the transistor needs to connect to the negative battery terminal.

To create these remaining connections, you can solder three small wires like this one to the circuit board as jumper wires:

Cut a piece of wire about 2 inches long and strip about 0.3 inches of insulation from both ends. Removing insulation from shorter wires can be tricky, so if you're struggling with this step, use a longer wire instead. When you know what length of wire you can strip most easily, prepare two more wires. Then, solder the three wires to make the remaining connections.

Run one wire from the base of the transistor to the upper pin of the potentiometer. Next, connect the one wire from the middle pin of the potentiometer to an empty row at the bottom of the board. Finally, run one wire from the same row of the prototyping board, where you just connected the previous wire, to the row connected to the emitter of the transistor. Check that your wires match the illustration and then solder them to the board.

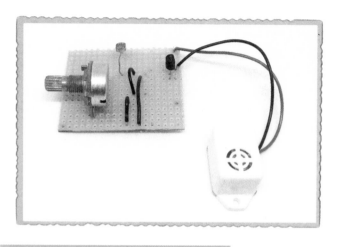

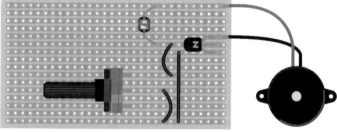

Step 5: Add the Battery Clip to the Board

All that's missing is the battery clip. Solder the battery clip's red wire to the top copper row of the board. The top row should also contain the photoresistor leg and the buzzer's red wire. Solder the battery clip's black wire to the bottom row.

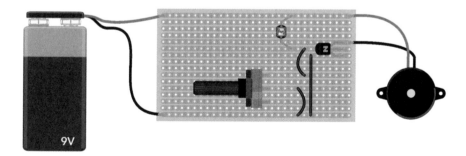

Step 6: Set a Wake-Up Call

Plug in the battery and put the circuit in an area that has the amount of light that you want to activate your alarm. Turn the shaft of the potentiometer until you find a position where the sound turns on and off with just a little nudge back and forth on the shaft. Now, turn the shaft just enough to make the sound turn on all the way. Place your hand over the photoresistor to block the light, and the sound should stop. Remove your hand, and the sound should turn on again.

Remove the battery from the circuit and wait until you're about to go to bed. With the lights off, place the circuit in your window, connect the battery, and go to sleep. When the sun rises and the light outside is as bright as the light you used to set your potentiometer, you'll be awakened by your very own sunrise alarm!

Step 7: What If There's No Sound?

Go through the circuit component by component, preferably with a friend. Check that your prototyping board has every connection shown in the circuit diagram. Check that there are no *short circuits*, too. A short circuit is an unintentional connection between something in a circuit. For example, make sure solder joints that are close to each other aren't actually touching.

If all looks good, use your multimeter to measure the voltage between the base and the emitter of the transistor. First, turn the shaft of your potentiometer all the way to one side, measure the voltage, and write it down. Then, turn the potentiometer all the way to the other side and measure the voltage again. Your multimeter should show 0 V on one side and around 0.7 V on the other side. If it doesn't, check your connections again.

If you're still not sure what's wrong, turn the potentiometer all the way to one side and measure the voltage between the red and black buzzer wires. Then, turn the potentiometer all the way to the other side and measure again. You should get 0 V on one side and about 8 to 9 V on the other.

If all else fails, check your solder joints and redo any that look like the connections might not be complete. And if you've built your circuit flawlessly, you may just have some broken components. Try breadboarding the project with new components, and if that works, solder those components instead.

TRY IT OUT: TEMPERATURE-CONTROLLED FAN

You can use the circuit you built in Project #15 for other things as well. For example, if you exchange the photoresistor for a *thermistor*, a resistor that changes resistance value based on temperature, the circuit will respond to temperature instead of light.

You can also change what's being controlled. Instead of an LED and resistor, try putting in a fan. Now you have a temperature-controlled fan! The circuit diagram looks like this:

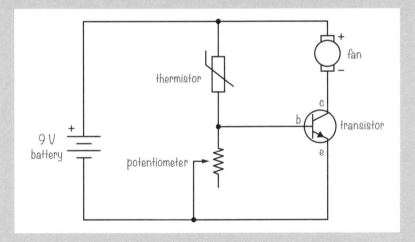

You'll need the following parts:

▶ **A standard 9 V battery** to power the circuit.

▶ **A 9 V battery clip** (Jameco #11280, Bitsbox #BAT033) to connect the battery to the circuit.

continued

- ▶ **A circuit board** (Jameco #2191488, Bitsbox #HW005) with copper strips.
- ▶ **Insulated wire** (Jameco #36792, Bitsbox #W106BK), about 10 inches in length. Standard hookup wire works fine.
- ▶ **A 10 kΩ thermistor** (Jameco #207037, Bitsbox #ST021)
- ▶ **A 10 kΩ potentiometer** (Jameco #2118791, Bitsbox #VR004)
- ▶ **A transistor PN2222A** (Jameco #178511, Bitsbox #QD101)
- ▶ **A 12 V DC fan** (Jameco #1708465, Bitsbox #AF002)

For this circuit, I've specified a different transistor. Different transistors can handle different amounts of current. A fan often draws much more current than the LED, so I've listed a transistor that can handle more current than the one you used previously.

To test the circuit, first use an ice cube to cool down the thermistor and then warm it up with your fingers to see the fan come on.

WHAT'S NEXT?

In this chapter, you learned how the most important component in electronics—the transistor—works. You also learned about the potentiometer and the photoresistor, and you combined these to build a sunrise wake-up alarm.

Now you've met almost all of the most common components used in electronics! And you've gotten some practice with soldering. In the following chapters, you're going to build circuits on a breadboard again because it's much easier to fix mistakes and reuse your components. If you want to make a permanent version of any of the circuits, just refer back to Chapter 6 on how to solder.

In Chapter 8, you'll learn about *integrated circuits*. These are small components that contain circuits that have been shrunk down to fit on a tiny chip. These chips can be used to create the most amazing types of circuits. You'll see what I mean when you build your very own electronic instrument in Chapter 8!

8

BUILDING A MUSICAL INSTRUMENT

This chapter will show you how to create sound with electronic components! Unlike other projects you've built so far, this chapter's projects use an *integrated circuit (IC)*, which is a whole circuit that's been shrunk down and packaged inside a tiny box. All sorts of circuits can be built as ICs, and most household devices are full of them. Peek inside a computer or an electronic toy, and you're sure to find a few.

To start, I'll explain what an IC is in more detail and describe how to figure out what a particular IC does. Then, you'll get some practice with ICs by building a simple circuit that makes some strange noises. At the end of the chapter, I'll show you how to build your very own electronic instrument that you can use to play music!

MEET THE INTEGRATED CIRCUIT

ICs are really small circuits that are conveniently packaged into little plastic boxes, which are often colored black. Any given IC has metal *pins* sticking out of it so you can connect other components to the circuit inside.

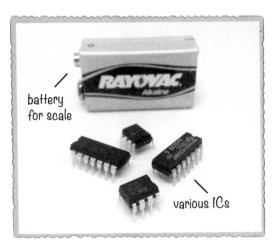

On the inside, an IC might contain a music player circuit, a radio circuit, a remote control circuit, or something else entirely. Because one little IC can contain a very complicated circuit, you can use ICs to make circuits with many different functions without building everything from scratch.

ICS AND DATASHEETS

Some ICs have only 8 pins, but other ICs have more than 100! To figure out what each pin on a specific IC does, you need to check that IC's datasheet, just as you did with the relay in "Project #11: Blink a Light!" on page 101. The datasheet tells you the function of each pin, and datasheets often show examples of how to use ICs in a circuit, too. To find a component's datasheet, try searching for the component name plus the term "datasheet" online, or check the website where you bought the component.

Datasheets often have tables with lots of numbers and technical terms, so the first time you see a datasheet for an IC, it might look very complex. But you usually don't need to read the whole datasheet. Instead, you can just look up the information you need and then go back to building your circuit.

HOW TO MAKE SOUND WITH ELECTRICITY

Sound is what you hear when air moves back and forth, or *vibrates*, really fast. Many devices that make noises, like the sound system in a car, do so with a *loudspeaker*, a component that vibrates air fast enough to make sound.

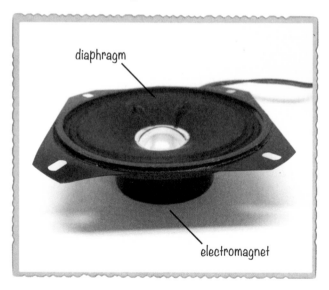

diaphragm

electromagnet

A loudspeaker has an electromagnet inside that moves a *diaphragm*, which is a surface that pushes the air in front of it. If a circuit turns the power to the loudspeaker's electromagnet on and off at, say, 1,000 times per second, then the diaphragm pushes the air back and forth 1,000 times per second. This is called the *frequency* of the sound, and frequency is measured in hertz (Hz). A frequency of 1,000 times per second, or 1,000 Hz, creates a steady beep.

SOUNDS THAT HUMANS CAN HEAR

Humans can hear sound only from around 20 Hz up to around 20,000 Hz. In "Project #11: Blink a Light!" on page 101, you built a circuit that blinked a light about once per second. If you had connected the output of the circuit to a speaker instead, the sound from the speaker would have a frequency of 1 Hz, which would be too low to hear. Instead, you would hear clicks from the speaker as it was switched on and off.

This means that to create sound you can hear, you need to create a circuit that can turn the voltage to a speaker on and off hundreds or thousands of times per second! Fortunately, there's an IC that can help you do just that.

MEET THE 555 TIMER

One classic IC is the *555 timer*, which you can use to switch things rapidly on and off. For example, you could use a 555 timer to blink a light every second, or you could connect it to a loudspeaker to make sound. Along with the 555 timer, you'd need to add a few extra resistors and capacitors, and by carefully selecting the values of those components, you could control how fast the light blinks or the sound's frequency. The 555 timer is very popular with hobbyists because it's cheap and pretty easy to use once you learn the basics. You'll use a 555 timer IC like the one shown here for the projects in this chapter.

part number

555 timer

Powering an IC

The datasheet for the 555 timer should tell you what each pin does. Try searching online for "555 timer datasheet" now. When you find the datasheet and open it, you should see a *pinout* like this:

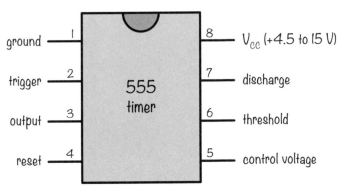

The 555 timer has eight pins. The pins of an IC are numbered counterclockwise, starting from the top left. (The top is indicated by a little notch or circle; some ICs have both.) The datasheet tells you the functions of each of the eight pins, but the following two pins are the most important to notice right now:

Pin 1, ground This pin must be connected to the negative terminal of your battery. Circuit diagrams that use ICs often label the negative battery terminal in a circuit schematic "ground," or GND for short.

Pin 8, V_{CC} This pin must be connected to the positive side of your battery, which must be at a voltage between 4.5 and 15 V. This means that a 9 V battery will work fine. On some ICs, this pin is called V_{DD} instead.

You'll find V_{CC} and ground pins on all ICs. They're the first pins to learn from any datasheet because you'll use them to power the circuit inside the IC.

The datasheet also shows how to connect the 555 timer in a circuit, and the circuit I find the most interesting connects the 555 timer in *astable mode*. *Astable* means that something is continually changing (not stable), and in astable mode, a 555 timer switches its output on and off constantly. That's perfect to blink a light or to create sound! Here's the circuit that tells the 555 timer to turn its output on and off:

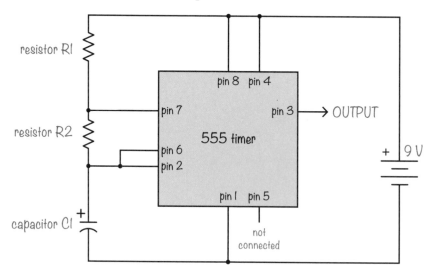

NOTE *The positions of the 555 pins have been arranged to suit the diagram; they're not in the same order as on the IC.*

How to Set the Output Speed of the 555 Timer

The values of R1, R2, and C1 in the circuit diagram determine how long the output pin stays *high*—meaning it outputs a voltage close to the battery voltage—and how long it stays *low*—meaning it outputs a voltage close to 0 V. The speed of the change in output, or the frequency, is the number of times the output goes from high to low in one second. When the 555 timer is connected in astable mode, as it is in the circuit diagram, the frequency of the output is controlled by resistors R1 and R2 and capacitor C1 according to the following formula:

$$\text{Frequency} = \frac{1.44}{(R1 + R2 + R2) \times C1}$$

Here, the resistor values are in ohms, and the capacitance is in farads. To find the frequency, first replace R1, R2, and C1 in the formula with the values of these parts and then punch the stuff on the right side of the equal sign into a calculator.

Let's try an example. Imagine a circuit with the following component values:

▶ R1 = 100 kΩ

▶ R2 = 10 kΩ

▶ C1 = 10 nF

What is the frequency of the output? Enter these values into the formula:

$$\text{Frequency} = \frac{1.44}{(100\ \text{k}\Omega + 10\ \text{k}\Omega + 10\ \text{k}\Omega) \times 10\ \text{nF}}$$

$$\text{Frequency} = \frac{1.44}{(120\ \text{k}\Omega) \times 10\ \text{nF}}$$

Now convert the units so the values are easier to multiply (120 kΩ = 120,000 Ω and 10 nF = 0.00000001 F):

$$\text{Frequency} = \frac{1.44}{120,000\ \Omega \times 0.00000001\ \text{F}}$$

$$\text{Frequency} = 1,200\ \text{Hz}$$

According to this calculation, the output should turn on and off 1,200 times per second with those values.

PROJECT #16: MAKE YOUR OWN SOUND WITH THE 555 TIMER

This project will show you how to play a sound with a frequency of about 1,200 Hz through a speaker. That's pretty cool! But a 1,200 Hz sound isn't very pleasant to listen to, and if you have any pets, they might appreciate the sound even less than you. In fact, when I turned on this circuit at my parents' home, their dog came running to me looking very confused and a bit scared. I turned it off quickly and moved my experiments to a place with no pets around, and I suggest not building this project around your pets, either.

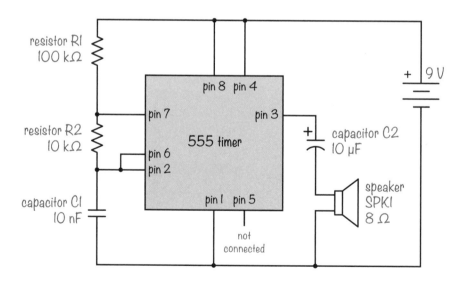

Shopping List

8 Ω speaker   breadboard

9 V battery

9 V battery clip

jumper wires

555 timer IC

10 nF capacitor

10 µF capacitor

100 kΩ and 10 kΩ resistors

▶ **A standard 9 V battery** to power the circuit.

▶ **A 9 V battery clip** (Jameco #11280, Bitsbox #BAT033) to connect the battery to the circuit.

▶ **A breadboard** (Jameco #20601, Bitsbox #CN329) with at least 30 rows.

▶ **Breadboard jumper wires** (Jameco #2237044, Bitsbox #CN236) for making easy connections. (Standard hookup wire works, too.)

▶ **A 555 timer IC** (Jameco #904085, Bitsbox #QU001) to create the timing.

▶ **A 8 Ω speaker** (Jameco #1954818, Bitsbox #ST063) to play the sound.

▶ **A 10 µF capacitor** (Jameco #29891, Bitsbox #EC10U25) to connect to the speaker.

- ▶ **A 10 nF capacitor** (Jameco #15229, Bitsbox #CC10N) to help set the frequency of the sound.
- ▶ **A 100 kΩ resistor** (Jameco #691340, Bitsbox #CR25100K) to help set the frequency of the sound.
- ▶ **A 10 kΩ resistor** (Jameco #691104, Bitsbox #CR2510K) to help set the frequency of the sound.

Step 1: Place the 555 Timer on the Breadboard

This circuit is built around the 555 timer IC, so first, place that IC in the middle of the breadboard, making it easy to connect all the components around it.

NOTE *When connecting an IC to a breadboard, always place it over the middle notch, with one set of pins on the left side and the other on the right side. Otherwise, any pins that share a row on the breadboard will be connected to each other.*

Place the IC's notch marker toward the top of the board so that pin 1 is at the upper-left corner and pin 8 is at the upper-right corner, as shown. Triple-check that you've oriented the chip as I describe; otherwise, the rest of the instructions in this project won't work.

Step 2: Set the Frequency

Next, connect the resistors and capacitor that set the frequency: R1, R2, and C1. The C1 capacitor isn't polarized, so it doesn't matter which way you connect it. Use the two vertical columns on the right for positive and negative: the red column for positive and the other for negative.

Connect R1, the 100 kΩ resistor, from pin 7 of the 555 timer to the positive column. Connect R2, the 10 kΩ resistor, from pin 6 to pin 7. And connect C1, the 10 nF capacitor, from pin 6 to the negative column. Then, connect a jumper wire from pin 2 to pin 6 to complete the rest of the connections that are needed to set the frequency.

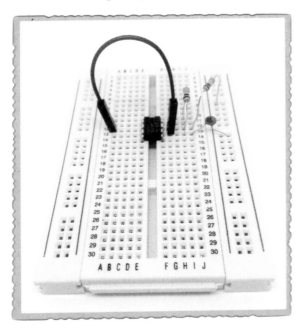

Step 3: Connect the Speaker and Coupling Capacitor

All the components to make the 555 timer output pin 3 turn on and off around 1,000 times per second should be in place on your breadboard now. If you were to connect the speaker directly to the output, a large current would flow through the speaker, possibly damaging both the speaker and the 555 IC. You could connect the speaker through a resistor to reduce the current, but using a capacitor is even better. When a capacitor is connected to an AC voltage, the capacitor acts a bit like a resistor, but if you connect it to a constant DC voltage, the current will be blocked. This means that there won't be any current running through the speaker unless there's actually a frequency to be played. When a capacitor is used like this, it's called a *coupling capacitor*.

The coupling capacitor for this project is a 10 µF polarized capacitor, so first identify which leg is negative. Connect the positive capacitor leg to the 555 timer's output pin 3. Then connect the capacitor's negative leg to an empty row on your breadboard.

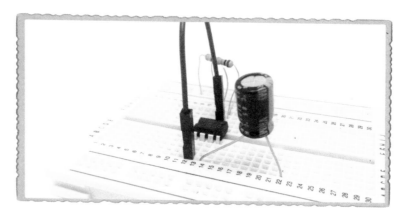

Next, if your speaker comes without wires, solder a wire about 6 inches long to each of the two contacts on the back of the speaker (ignore any + or − labels by the speaker contacts). Then, connect one of the speaker wires to the same row as the negative capacitor leg and the other wire to the negative supply column.

Step 4: Connect the Power and Reset Pins

Compare your breadboard to the circuit diagram at the beginning of the project, and you'll see that there are a few connections missing. Once you have all of your components in place on the breadboard, you can make those final connections with jumper wires. Add a jumper wire for each of the following connections:

▶ From pin 1 on the 555 timer to the negative supply column

▶ From pin 8 on the 555 timer to the positive supply column

▶ From pin 4 on the 555 timer to the positive supply column

Note that there's no connection to pin 5 of the 555 timer in this circuit.

Step 5: Make Some Sound!

Connect the battery clip to your supply columns on the right side of the breadboard. The red wire goes to the positive supply column, and the black wire goes to the negative supply column.

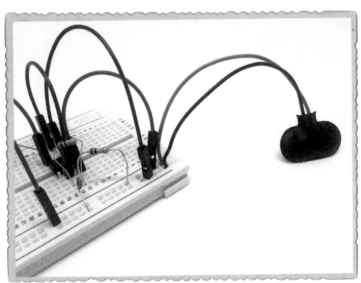

When you're ready, connect the battery, and you should hear a loud beep. Congratulations: You just made your first electronic sound!

Step 6: What If There's No Sound?

There are a lot of connections in this circuit, so if your circuit doesn't work on your first attempt, don't worry: that happens to everyone who plays with electronics at some point. First, disconnect the battery, and then check the resistor and capacitor legs. These legs are long, and they can easily end up in contact with each other by accident, creating a short circuit. (For example, if you accidentally connect the positive terminal of the battery directly to the negative terminal, that short-circuits the battery.)

Next, check the component connections to the 555 timer. The 555 timer's pins must connect to the rest of the circuit according to the circuit diagram, or the IC won't work. When there are a lot of connections, it's easy to plug a wire into the wrong row of the breadboard.

CHECKING CONNECTIONS AS A TEAM

Finding circuit problems is called *debugging*, and it's easier to do with some help. When you get stuck, ask someone else to look at the circuit diagram and say the connections out loud one by one while you check the real connections. For example, if your friend is reading the schematic and you're looking at the breadboard, you might have a conversation like this:

> Friend: "The positive side of the battery is connected to one side of R1."
>
> You: "Got it!"
>
> Friend: "The positive side of the battery is also connected to pins 4 and 8 of the IC."
>
> You: "Got it!"
>
> Friend: "The other side of R1 is connected to pin 7 of the chip and to one side of the resistor R2."
>
> You: "Oh, wait! I don't have the connection to pin 7!"

And just like that, you'll discover the problem.

If all your components appear to be oriented correctly and you see no short circuits, then check all your breadboard connections to make sure components that should be connected share a row. Start with the connection from the positive terminal of the battery on your circuit diagram. Is it connected on the board just as the circuit diagram shows? If yes, then move on to the next connection; keep going like this until you've checked all the connections.

TURNING AN ANNOYING BEEP INTO MUSIC

The sound you created in the previous project isn't very pleasant. So how can you turn it into music? Musical notes are just sound waves that vibrate at specific frequencies, and that means it's possible to make an electronic instrument with the 555 timer. If you change the frequency of the signal that goes into the speaker, then the tone of the sound will change. You just have to find a way to change the 555 timer's output frequency at will, without rebuilding the circuit every time.

Chapter 7 introduced two components that can change their resistance value: the potentiometer and the photoresistor. If you use one of those components to control the frequency of the 555 timer's output signal, then when that component's resistance changes, the sound will change, too. That's how you'll make the instrument in the next project.

PROJECT #17: AN INSTRUMENT THAT BEEPS AND BOOPS

This project shows you how to combine what you've learned so far to build your very own electronic instrument. Specifically, you're going to build an instrument with a button to play sound and a potentiometer shaft to change the tone.

This instrument is like a very simple *synthesizer* that uses electricity to make sounds. Synthesizers have been used to add all kinds of bleeps, bloops, and glitchy sounds to songs since the beginning of the electronic music genre. This one is pretty basic, but it still makes plenty of fun noises. In fact, the circuit for this project looks very similar to the circuit from "Project #16: Make Your Own Sound with the 555 Timer" on page 167, but it has a few twists.

This circuit replaces the separate R1 and R2, which the circuits in Project #16 used, with a potentiometer (and a protective 1 kΩ resistor). The potentiometer acts like two resistors, meaning that you can effectively change the values of R1 and R2 whenever you want to change the tone you hear.

Notice that this circuit also has a switch connected to the positive battery terminal. This switch is a push button, and with a switch between power and your circuit, the instrument should make a sound only when you push the button.

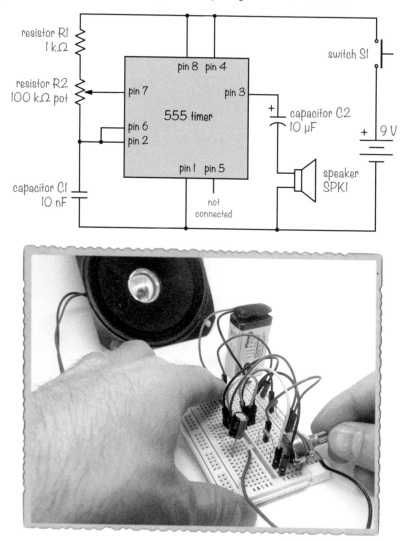

Shopping List

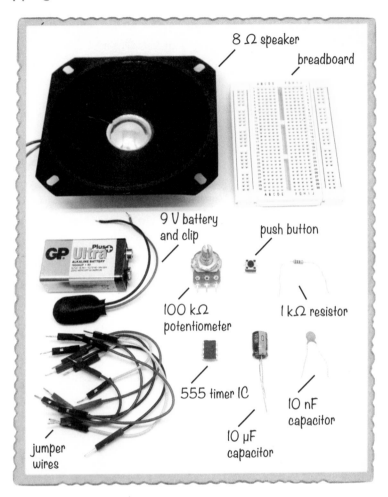

- ▶ **A standard 9 V battery** to power the circuit.
- ▶ **A 9 V battery clip** (Jameco #11280, Bitsbox #BAT033) to connect the battery to the circuit.
- ▶ **A breadboard** (Jameco #20601, Bitsbox #CN329) with at least 30 rows.
- ▶ **Breadboard jumper wires** (Jameco #2237044, Bitsbox #CN236) for making easy connections. (Standard hookup wire works, too.)
- ▶ **A 555 timer IC** (Jameco #904085, Bitsbox #QU001) to create the timing.

- **A 8 Ω speaker** (Jameco #1954818, Bitsbox #ST063) to play the sound.
- **A 10 µF capacitor** (Jameco #29891, Bitsbox #EC10U25) to connect to the speaker.
- **A 10 nF capacitor** (Jameco #15229, Bitsbox #CC10N) to help set the frequency of the sound.
- **A 100 kΩ potentiometer** (Jameco #2161406, Bitsbox #VR006) to control the tone.
- **A 1 kΩ resistor** (Jameco #690865, Bitsbox #CR251K) to protect pin 7 from being connected directly to V_{CC}.
- **A push button** (Jameco #119011, Bitsbox #SW087) to play tones with.

Step 1: Connect the 555 Timer and the Capacitors

Start by connecting the 555 timer in the middle of the board. Then, connect both capacitors. Connect C1, the 10 nF capacitor, from pin 6 to the negative power column. And connect C2, the 10µF capacitor, with its positive leg at pin 3 of the chip and the negative leg on an empty row farther down. When you're done, your board should look something like this:

Step 2: Connect Jumper Wires

Use jumper wires to create the following connections:

- Pin 8 to the breadboard's positive supply column
- Pin 4 to the breadboard's positive supply column
- Pin 1 to the breadboard's negative supply column
- Pin 2 to pin 6

Step 3: Connect the Note Controller and Resistor

Next up is the potentiometer, which controls the note that plays. Because it takes up more space, plug this in at the bottom of the breadboard, as shown, and be sure each leg is in its own row.

Connect the 1 kΩ resistor from the uppermost leg of the potentiometer to an unused row away from the 555 IC and connect a jumper wire from this row to the positive supply. Then, connect one jumper wire to each of the two remaining potentiometer legs. Connect the wire on the middle potentiometer leg to pin 7 on the 555 timer, and connect the wire on the lower leg to pin 6 on the 555 timer.

Step 4: Add the "On" Button

You're almost done! Instead of wiring the battery clip directly to the positive supply column on the breadboard, you're going to connect it through a push button, which will act as an "on" button for your instrument. This way, the circuit will get power from the battery only when the button is pushed and, therefore, make sound only when you push the button.

The push button in the Shopping List (page 177) has four pins, but the two legs in the front are connected and the two pins in the back are connected. That means this button works exactly like a two-pin switch. When you push the button, you connect the front pair of pins with the back pair. Your circuit will get power and you'll hear the sound. When you release the button, the circuit loses power again and the sound will stop.

push button

Plug the push button into your breadboard over the notch in the middle. Then, use a jumper wire to connect one side of the push button to the breadboard's positive supply column. Next, connect the positive wire from your battery clip to the other side of the push button. Finally, connect the negative battery clip wire to the negative supply column.

Step 5: Add the Loudspeaker

Connect one of the speaker wires to the same row as the negative capacitor leg and the other wire to the negative supply column.

Step 6: Play Some Music!

Connect your battery to the battery clip and push the button. Did you hear a sound? Try turning the potentiometer spindle back and forth until you hear something.

You can make a beat by pushing the button in any rhythm you like, and you can control the tone by turning the shaft of the potentiometer in between. Beep, baap, booop!

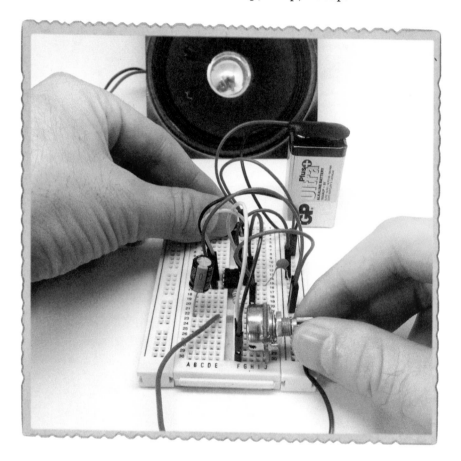

Step 7: What If the Instrument Doesn't Work?

Some potentiometers aren't perfectly fitted for breadboards, so start by checking whether your potentiometer is properly connected to the breadboard. Next, check that the two capacitors and the push button are connected according to the circuit diagram at the beginning of the project.

There are a lot of wires on this board, so it's easy to mix up connections. If you still aren't able to hear any sound, then go through all the connections on your board and check that they're correct. I suggest using the process I described in "Checking Connections as a Team" on page 174.

TRY IT OUT: MAKE A MOTION-CONTROLLED INSTRUMENT

Instead of replacing both R1 and R2 with a potentiometer, try using a 1 kΩ resistor for R1 and a photoresistor for R2, as shown in this circuit diagram. As you move your hand over the photoresistor, the amount of light hitting it should change, and the instrument should play different notes!

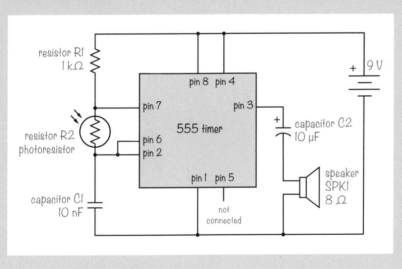

WHAT'S NEXT?

There are millions of integrated circuits in the world, and they do all kinds of awesome things. Remember, whenever you want to use an IC in your projects, you can use its datasheet to find out both what the IC does and what kind of circuit you need to make it work.

In this chapter, you learned how to use a 555 timer IC to make music. These circuits had lots of connections, so if you didn't get them right the first time, then you're in good company. Most people mix up wires the first time they connect a circuit, and fixing the connections is great practice! And speaking of practice, now would be a good time to do some more soldering. Why not solder your instrument on to a prototyping board—and maybe even put it in a box?

Integrated circuits are very commonly used in *digital circuits*. Digital circuits can do many things simply by switching the right parts on and off, often very rapidly, just as in the musical instrument you made in this chapter. Modern gadgets like your computer use digital circuits, and you'll learn more about digital electronics in the last few chapters of this book.

PART 3

THE DIGITAL WORLD

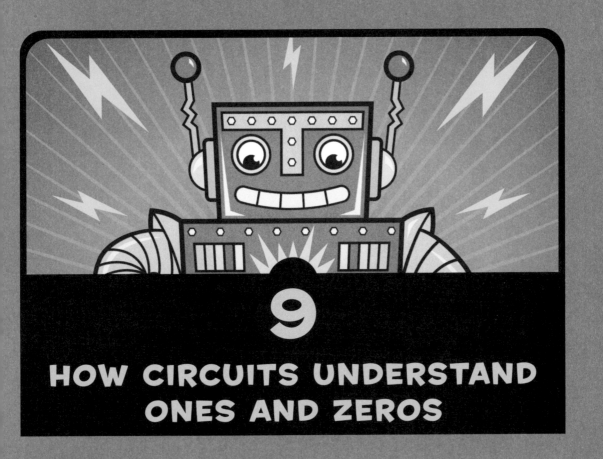

9

HOW CIRCUITS UNDERSTAND ONES AND ZEROS

obile phones, computers, TVs, video game consoles, and almost all the other technology you see around you is built with digital electronics. If you've ever looked inside a computer, the circuits might seem complex, but when you break that hardware down into small pieces, it's actually quite simple: every action a computer takes is based on whether some circuit sees a high or low voltage.

You've used transistors to make circuits that control things, and in this chapter, you'll learn the basics of using digital electronics to make even smarter circuits. You're going to learn a new number system, what bits and bytes are, and how you can use bits and bytes to create messages with electricity.

ONES AND ZEROS AS VOLTAGES

When I was in school, my teacher told me that computers used ones and zeros to communicate, but he didn't explain it any further. I wanted to know more, so I decided to ask my dad. Because computers are complex machines, I assumed the way they use ones and zeros was going to be complex, too, but my dad told me, "In a computer, a one is just a wire with voltage, and a zero is a wire without voltage." (By "without voltage," my dad meant the voltage was zero.)

In "How to Set the Output Speed of the 555 Timer" on page 166, I mentioned briefly that the pins of the 555 timer could be either high or low. The pins on the ICs in a computer work the same way: high is one, and low is zero. Digital circuits work by flipping the voltages on different wires between high and low.

MEET THE BINARY NUMBER SYSTEM

Normally, when you talk about numbers, you use *decimal numbers*, which are in the *base-10* number system. In base-10 numbers, a digit can have one of 10 possible values, from 0 to 9. But digital circuits can work with only two voltages (high and low), so they can understand only *binary numbers*. Binary is also called the *base-2* number system, and a binary number's digits have only two possible values: 0 and 1.

Here's how you'd count to 10 in both decimal and binary:

Decimal number	Binary number
0	0
1	1
2	10
3	11
4	100
5	101
6	110
7	111
8	1000
9	1001
10	1010

What's going on here? The number 2 in decimal is 10 in binary, and 4 in decimal is 100 in binary!

You can figure out the value of any number in any system using the digits and their position. The rightmost digit always gets multiplied by 1. Going left from there, each position's value equals the base times the value of the previous position. In decimal, the base is 10, so the second position's value is 10, or 10 × 1; the third position's value is 100, or 10 × 10; the fourth position's value is 1000, or 10 × 100; and so on. Here's an example:

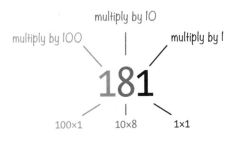

$$100 + 80 + 1 = 181$$

In the number 181, the first digit is 1, the second digit is 8, and the third digit is 1. Once you multiply those digits by their position values, you can add the resulting values to get 181. You don't need to use this method to figure out decimal numbers, though. It's pretty clear that 181 equals 181! But this method is very useful for finding the value of binary numbers. Binary follows the same rules, but it uses a base of 2 instead.

PROJECT #18: CONVERT FROM BINARY TO DECIMAL

In this project, you're going to *convert* a binary number into its decimal form. Converting a number to a different base just means calculating that number's value and writing it using digits in the new base.

Tools

▸ **A pen or pencil** to write with.
▸ **Paper** to write on.
▸ **A calculator** to add numbers. If you're good at doing math in your head, try this project without one.

Step 1: Write It Down on Paper

First, write an eight-digit binary number on paper, leaving space between the digits, both above and below the number. I'm going to convert the binary number 1011 0101, and I wrote it out like this:

1 0 1 1 0 1 0 1

Step 2: Write the Position Values

Next, write the value of each position above each digit. Binary works the same way as the decimal example, but the base is 2. That means the value for the rightmost position is 1, and to find the next position to the left, you'd multiply the previous position's value by 2. For example, the second position's value is $2 \times 1 = 2$; the third position's value is $2 \times 2 = 4$; the fourth value is $4 \times 2 = 8$; and so on. Use a calculator if you don't want to calculate it all in your head. When you write those values down, you should have something like this:

position values	128	64	32	16	8	4	2	1
digits	1	0	1	1	0	1	0	1

Step 3: Find the Value of Each Digit

Look at each digit of the binary number you wrote down. If a digit is 0, write 0 below it. If the digit is 1, write the value of that position below it. Those are the values you'll add together to get your final decimal number.

position values	128	64	32	16	8	4	2	1
digits	1	0	1	1	0	1	0	1
values to add	128	0	32	16	0	4	0	1

Step 4: Add the Numbers

You should now have three rows of numbers. Add the numbers in the bottom row (you might find it helpful to write a + sign between each pair of numbers) to get the sum, which is the decimal value of your binary number.

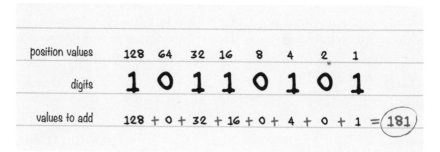

position values	128	64	32	16	8	4	2	1
digits	1	0	1	1	0	1	0	1
values to add	128 +	0 +	32 +	16 +	0 +	4 +	0 +	1 = (181)

The binary number 1011 0101 is 181 in decimal. If you've been following along with that number and your answer is different, go through the steps again and check your results against mine to find out where the error is.

TRY IT OUT:
TRANSFORM MORE BINARY NUMBERS

To get more practice with ones and zeros, let's bring some more binary numbers into the decimal world. Here are a few to try:*

1010

0011 1111

1000 0000

0011 1011 0101

---

* In decimal, these binary numbers are 10, 63, 128, and 949.

BITS AND BYTES

Each digit in a binary number is called a *bit* (that's short for *binary digit*), and computers handle numbers in blocks of eight bits called a *byte*. The binary number 1011 0101 has eight bits, so it's a byte. You can interact with a computer in many ways, but all your mouse clicks, key presses, webcam videos, and so on need to be translated into bits and bytes before the computer can understand them.

In fact, when working with computers and other digital gadgets, you usually see much, much larger numbers than just 1 byte. All the files on a computer are collections of bytes, but if you tried to describe their size in bytes alone, those numbers would be huge! That's why files are usually described in larger units, like kilobytes* (kB), megabytes (MB), gigabytes (GB), terabytes (TB), and so on. Here's what those units mean:

1 kB = 1,000 bytes

1 MB = 1,000 kB = 1,000,000 bytes

1 GB = 1,000 MB = 1,000,000 kB = 1,000,000,000 bytes

1 TB = 1,000 GB = 1,000,000 MB = 1,000,000,000 kB
       = 1,000,000,000,000 bytes

If a computer's hard disk can hold 1 TB of data, then it can hold one trillion bytes, which is eight trillion ones and zeros!

NUMBERS CAN BE ANYTHING

Now you might be thinking, "Why on Earth would I ever need eight trillion ones and zeros in my computer?" The fact is, whether you use a computer to write stories, draw pictures, talk to your friends, play video games, or anything else, you're actually using those ones and zeros.

For example, how does a computer show an image on a screen? A computer screen is made of a lot of small points called *pixels*, and each pixel can be set to a color that is a mix of red, green, and blue light. If you want a pixel to be

---

* Sometimes kilobyte refers to 1024 bytes (2^{10}).

the brightest yellow possible, you'd use numbers to tell the computer to turn that pixel's red and green settings to full intensity and its blue setting to zero (because mixed red and green light looks like yellow). This way you can translate numbers into an image on the screen.

PROJECT #19: COLOR GUESSING GAME

In this project, you'll build a pixel-color guessing game using binary values. It's a two-player game where you and a friend take turns being "the computer" and "the user."

The person who is the computer sets the color of the pixel by pushing a combination of three buttons. When the computer is ready, the user must try to guess which color the pixel is. When the user is ready to make the guess, they should say the chosen color out loud and then push the color revealer button to show the actual color. If the user guesses correctly, they get one point and get to guess again. If the guess is wrong, you switch roles. The first one to reach three points wins the round.

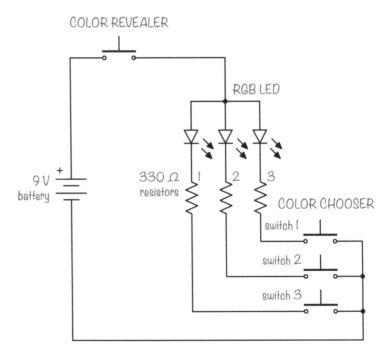

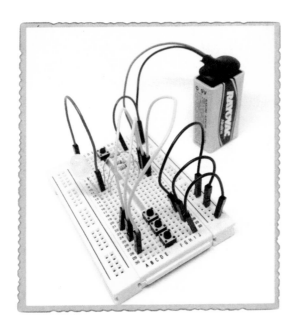

Meet the RGB LED

To create the pixel for this project, you're going to use a *red-green-blue (RGB) LED*, which combines a red LED, a green LED, and a blue LED into one component. By turning on and off each of these LEDs, you can create different colors. For example, turning on only the red and green LEDs would give you yellow.

There are two types of RGB LEDs: *common anode* and *common cathode*. This is what a common anode RGB LED looks like, along with its symbol:

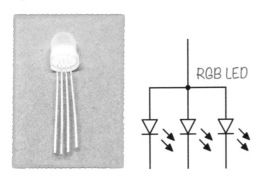

RGB LEDs have four legs. You'll use three legs to set the color, and the fourth leg is the *common* leg. In common anode RGB LEDs, the positive (anode) sides of the three LEDs are combined into one pin; common cathode RGBs combine the negative (cathode) sides into one pin.

In this project, you're going to build the following circuit, which uses a common anode RGB LED and some buttons.

Shopping List

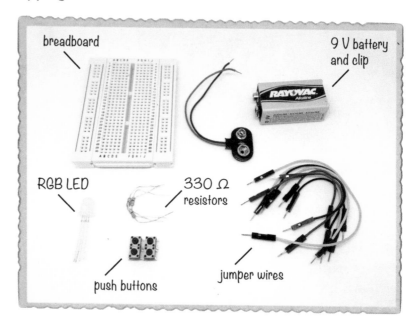

- ▶ **A standard 9 V battery** to power the circuit.
- ▶ **A 9 V battery clip** (Jameco #11280, Bitsbox #BAT033) to connect the battery to the circuit.
- ▶ **A breadboard** (Jameco #20601, Bitsbox #CN329) with at least 30 rows.
- ▶ **Breadboard jumper wires** (Jameco #2237044, Bitsbox #CN236) to easily connect parts. (Standard hookup wire works, too.)
- ▶ **Three 330 Ω resistors** (Jameco #661386, Bitsbox #CR25330R) for limiting the current to the LED.

- **RGB LED with common anode** (Jameco #2219567, Bitsbox #OP100) to create colors.
- **Four push buttons** (Jameco #119011, Bitsbox #SW087) to set and reveal colors.

Step 1: Place the Color Chooser's Push Buttons

Orient your breadboard so that the notch down the middle runs from top to bottom. Then, place three push buttons at the bottom of your breadboard; each should have one pair of legs on the left side of the notch and one pair on the right. This should leave you plenty of room to connect components on both sides of the buttons, and you'll be able to separate the computer's buttons from the user's button more easily. With your buttons in position, connect three jumper wires from the bottom-right pin of each push button to the negative supply column.

bottom-right pin

Step 2: Connect the RGB LED

In the middle of the board on the left, connect your RGB LED. The longest leg of the RGB LED is the common anode leg. Leave this unconnected for now. Connect a 330 Ω resistor from each of the remaining LED legs to an empty row on the right side of the breadboard. From each of these three rows, connect a jumper wire to the top-left pin of each push button.

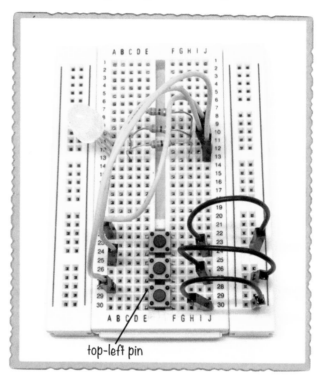

top-left pin

Step 3: Connect the Color Revealer Button

Next, add the button that reveals the computer's chosen color to the user. Place a fourth push button all the way at the top of the breadboard, across the middle notch. Connect a jumper wire from the common anode leg of the RGB LED to the top-left pin of the fourth push button. Then, connect one jumper wire from the bottom-right pin of this push button to the positive supply column on the right.

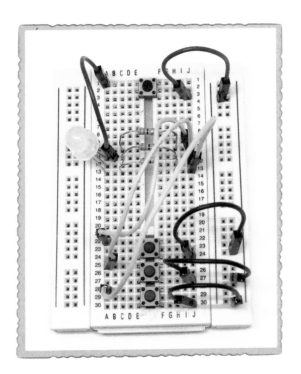

Step 4: Test the Colors

Connect the battery clip to the supply columns on the right, connect a battery, and try it out! Push some of the buttons on the bottom and then push the color revealer button to see the color. In this photo, I set my RGB LED to green.

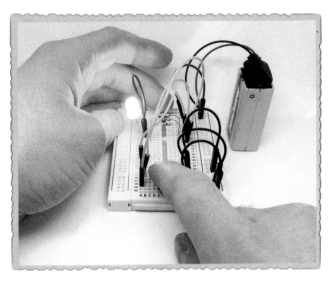

You should be able to see the following seven colors, depending on which buttons you push:

Color	Top button	Middle button	Lower button
Red	Pushed (1)	Not pushed (0)	Not pushed (0)
Green	Not pushed (0)	Pushed (1)	Not pushed (0)
Blue	Not pushed (0)	Not pushed (0)	Pushed (1)
Yellow	Pushed (1)	Pushed (1)	Not pushed (0)
Cyan	Not pushed (0)	Pushed (1)	Pushed (1)
Magenta	Pushed (1)	Not pushed (0)	Pushed (1)
White	Pushed (1)	Pushed (1)	Pushed (1)

If your buttons do not match these colors, switch the wires between the three resistors to the buttons so that they match.

Step 5: What If the Game Doesn't Work?

If you see no colors at all, check that your connections match the circuit diagram. If the connections are correct and you still can't see any colors when pushing the color revealer button, you may have a common cathode LED instead of a common anode. To check for this, simply switch the positive and negative connections from the battery.

When you've verified that all the colors work, invite a friend to play!

> **TRY IT OUT:**
> **SOLDER THE COLOR GUESSING GAME**
>
> This is a perfect circuit to practice your soldering skills on. Get a prototyping board and solder the circuit onto it so that you have a permanent Color Guessing Game to bring with you on a long car ride.

HOW BINARY NUMBERS CAN CREATE WORDS

Images aren't the only things that can be stored as binary numbers; you can represent letters as numbers, too. One way to do this is to use the *ASCII code*, which is a standard set of bytes that computers understand as upper- and lowercase letters, numbers, punctuation marks, and so on. The numbers in this table represent the lowercase letters in the English alphabet.

Decimal ASCII code	Binary value	Lowercase letter
97	0110 0001	a
98	0110 0010	b
99	0110 0011	c
100	0110 0100	d
101	0110 0101	e
102	0110 0110	f
103	0110 0111	g
104	0110 1000	h
105	0110 1001	i
106	0110 1010	j
107	0110 1011	k
108	0110 1100	l
109	0110 1101	m
110	0110 1110	n
111	0110 1111	o
112	0111 0000	p
113	0111 0001	q
114	0111 0010	r
115	0111 0011	s
116	0111 0100	t
117	0111 0101	u
118	0111 0110	v
119	0111 0111	w
120	0111 1000	x
121	0111 1001	y
122	0111 1010	z

For example, the letter *a* can be represented by the decimal number 97, which is the binary number 0110 0001. You can use this table to encode and decode secret messages written with only ones and zeros.

PROJECT #20: THE SECRET MESSAGE MACHINE

This project is a circuit that shows eight-bit binary numbers with LEDs. An LED that is lit is a 1, and an LED that is off is a 0. You'll use switches to set the binary number and a push button to show the binary number on the LEDs.

Eight bits are enough to represent an ASCII character, so you can use this project to generate secret messages that can only be decoded by someone who knows binary! This finished Secret Message Machine shows the letter *w*, or 0111 0111.

O111 O111

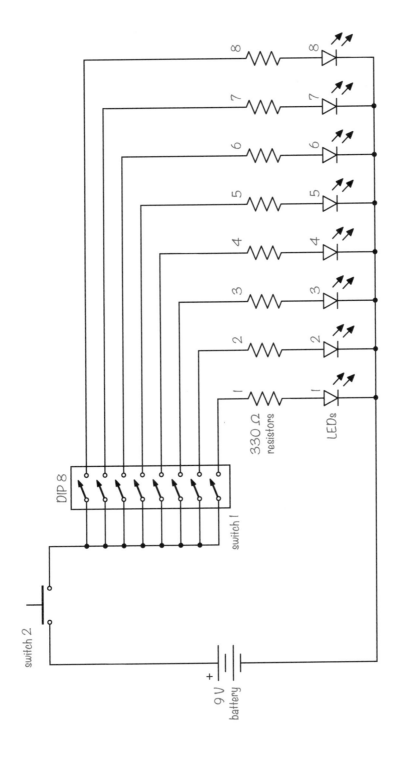

Meet the DIP Switch

This circuit uses eight switches to set the binary value, but it would be a pain to plug that many individual buttons into your breadboard. Fortunately, you can just use a *DIP switch*, which is a component with a row of one or more mini switches.

NOTE   *DIP stands for* dual in-line package, *which is how the pins are arranged. A component with "DIP" in its name has two rows of pins that you can plug into a breadboard. The DIP switch in this project has eight individual switches. This is perfect for creating a binary value input to a row of LEDs.*

Shopping List

▶ **A standard 9 V battery** to power the circuit.

▶ **A 9 V battery clip** (Jameco #11280, Bitsbox #BAT033) to connect the battery to the circuit.

▶ **A breadboard** (Jameco #20601, Bitsbox #CN329) with at least 30 rows.

▶ **Breadboard jumper wires** (Jameco #2237044, Bitsbox #CN236) to easily connect parts. (Standard hookup wire works, too.)

▶ **Eight 330 Ω resistors** (Jameco #661386, Bitsbox #CR25330R) for limiting the current to the LEDs. Any value between 270 Ω and 470 Ω works well.

- **Eight blue LEDs** (Jameco #2193889, Bitsbox #OP033) to show the binary number.
- **One 8-position DIP switch** (Jameco #696984, Bitsbox #SW098) to set the binary number.
- **A push button** (Jameco #119011, Bitsbox #SW087) to turn on the LEDs.

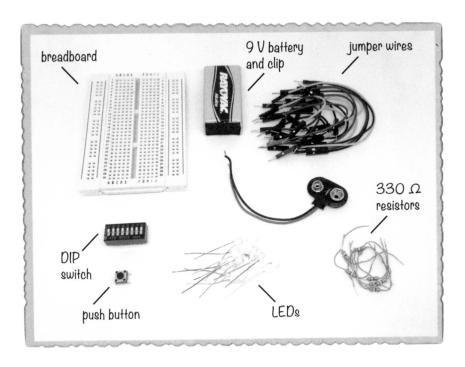

Step 1: Connect the Push Button

Plug the push button into the top of your breadboard. This project will take up a lot of space on your breadboard, so from here on, try to keep your components as close together as possible.

Connect a jumper wire from the top-right breadboard row, which should be connected to the upper pin of the push button, to the positive supply rail on the right side. Then, connect a jumper wire from the lower pin to the positive supply column on the left.

Your breadboard should look something like this:

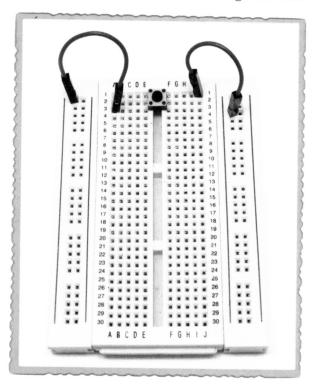

This push button controls the connection from the battery's positive terminal to the rest of the circuit. When the button is not pushed, there's no closed loop for the current to flow through, and the circuit doesn't have power.

Step 2: Connect the DIP Switch

Next, connect the DIP switch to your breadboard just below the push button, with the numbers on the right side of the middle notch. Run one jumper wire from each of the eight rows to the positive supply column on the left, for a total of eight wires. You'll need to be able to set the switches on and off, so connect the wires as far away from the switch as possible to leave room for your fingers.

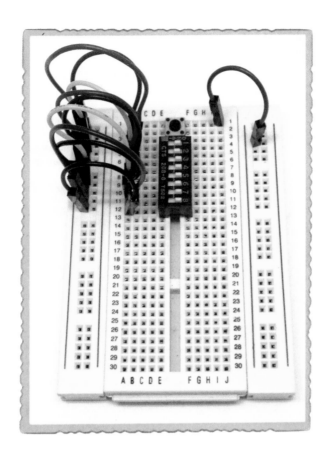

Step 3: Connect the LEDs

Now, connect one LED's short leg to the negative supply column on the right, and connect its long leg to the last row at the bottom of your breadboard. Follow the same pattern upward to plug the rest of the LEDs into the breadboard on rows of their own, leaving one empty row between LEDs. (If you want to make it easier to read the LEDs, put your LEDs in two groups of four by leaving a couple of extra rows after the fourth LED.) Then, connect a resistor from each row with an LED to the same row on the left side of the notch in the middle of the breadboard.

It will be best to connect the LEDs and switches so that you and your friend can sit on opposite sides of the board and see the bits in the same order, so pay careful attention to these connections. With your resistors in place, connect a jumper wire from each resistor row on the left side of the breadboard notch to a DIP-switch pin on the right side of the notch. Connect the resistor closest to the bottom of the breadboard to Switch 1, the next LED to Switch 2, and so on; you should end by connecting the top resistor to Switch 8.

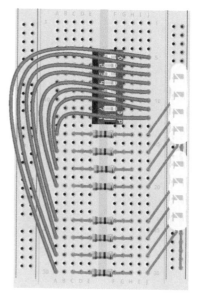

Step 4: Send a Secret Message!

Connect the negative side of the battery clip to the negative supply column, and then connect the positive side to the positive supply column, as shown.

Then, push all the switches in the "on" direction, press and hold the button to see whether all the lights light up, and turn off each LED one by one.

If all the LEDs work, it's time to play! Invite a friend over and use this circuit to "talk" to them without speaking. Sit on opposite sides of a table, write down a word on a piece of paper for your own reference, and keep it hidden from your friend. Look at the ASCII code table and set the switches to the binary values for the first letter in your word. For example, the switch in the next photo is set to display a lowercase letter *a*.

O110 O001

When your switch bank is ready to show a letter, push the button so that the LEDs light up. Hold the push button while your friend writes down the binary value. Then, release the push button and set the binary value for the next character. Keep doing this until you've shown all the characters in your word. When you're done, show the ASCII code table to your friend so they can try to figure out your word.

Step 5: What If the Secret Message Machine Doesn't Work?

If you've been following along for the whole book, you've connected a lot of LED circuits, but this one does have a lot of components. It's easy to make a wrong connection somewhere, so if your circuit doesn't work right away, check each connection carefully against this project's circuit diagram.

If none of the lights work, first check that the battery's positive and negative terminals are connected correctly. Next, check that the LEDs are oriented the right way and that the resistors are the right values. If some lights work while others don't, then some of the LED or resistor legs may be touching when they shouldn't. Inspect them closely to find the error.

WHY COMPUTERS USE ONES AND ZEROS

Computers use ones and zeros instead of the decimal numbers from 0 to 9 because when you have only two values, it makes constructing electronic circuits to do calculations and store the values much easier.

For example, because each digit has only two possible values, one or zero, it's easy to create a simple memory block to store binary numbers using switches, as you did with the DIP switch in Project #20.

It's possible to save ones and zeros in many different ways, thereby creating *memory*. In the early days of computing, it was common to save sets of ones and zeros as physical cards with holes in them. Today, many hard disks save ones and zeros on magnetic disks, or even via electrons stored inside an integrated circuit.

WHAT'S NEXT?

In this chapter, you learned how binary numbers work. You've seen how ones and zeros can be used to show images on your computer screen and how to decode a bunch of seemingly random ones and zeros into readable text. To explore binary numbers a bit more, come up with your own binary codes for the letters in the alphabet. There are 26 letters from a to z. How many digits do you need to represent all 26 letters? To figure this out, you can start by saying that the binary number 1 means a. The next binary number, 10, is b. Next, 11, is c. Write this down and keep increasing until you reach z. Then, count the number of digits you needed for the z. This is the minimum number of digits you need.

Here's another thing to try. Normally, if you count with your fingers, you can count to 10, right? If you don't use your thumbs, you can only count to 8. But what if you count in binary instead? A straight finger is 1, and a bent finger is 0. How high can you count with eight fingers now?

Digital values have another very important use: they allow you to create *logic circuits*, which make decisions based on whether certain wires see a high voltage or a low voltage. High is typically considered "true," and low is typically "false." If those wires are associated with simple true-or-false questions and the voltages are the answers, then you can think of the output from a logic circuit as a conclusion reached after asking a series of questions.

With logic, you can make circuits that do math, like adding two numbers, or circuits that do something only under a certain condition, like a door lock that opens only if you input the right combination of numbers. In Chapter 10, I'll show you some of the building blocks of digital logic and how you can make smart circuits with them.

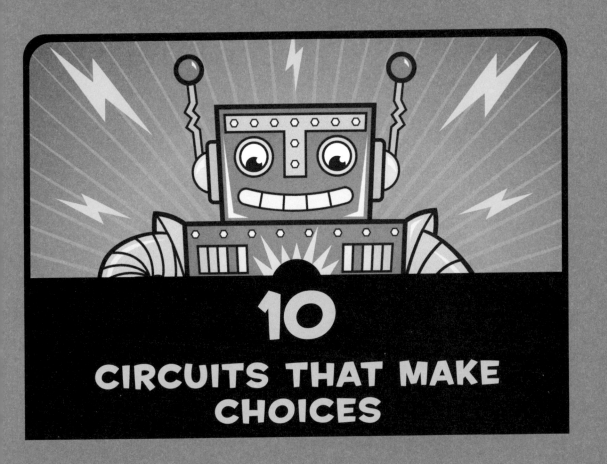

10

CIRCUITS THAT MAKE CHOICES

hapter 9 was all about ones and zeros, and you played with bits and bytes in a couple of projects. Now in this chapter, you'll make circuits that actually use ones and zeros to make decisions. *Logic gates* are components that check for the voltages that represent those ones and zeros and output a voltage accordingly. I'll show you a few types of logic gates and how you can use them to create a secret code detector.

IT'S ONLY LOGICAL

Logic is a way of reaching a conclusion based on pieces of information that you know to be true or false. For example, imagine you know the following statement is true, beyond a doubt:

> Statement 1: IF there are oranges in your fridge AND you have an orange squeezer, THEN you're able to make orange juice.

If you trust the preceding statement, then there are two conditions to check before you can make orange juice:

> Condition 1: There are oranges in your fridge.
>
> Condition 2: You have an orange squeezer.

If you check your kitchen and find that these conditions are true, then you can logically conclude that you can make orange juice.

Computers use *Boolean logic*, which is a system of logic that works only with the values *true* and *false* to convert ones and zeros into actions. For a computer to know whether you can make orange juice or not, it would have to reach that conclusion through Boolean logic. Let's try thinking like a computer!

First, look for the conditions in Statement 1 that affect whether you can make orange juice or not. In this case, the conditions are the two phrases between "if" and "then," joined by "and." Assign them letters as follows:

> There are oranges in your fridge. = A
>
> You have an orange squeezer. = B

The conclusion is the statement after "then." Give it a letter, too:

You're able to make orange juice. = Q

With these letters, you could rewrite Statement 1 as "If A and B, then Q." In Boolean logic shorthand, that looks like this:

A AND B = Q

This is a *logic equation*, where *AND* is an operator like addition or subtraction. When both statements on either side of AND are true, the conclusion Q is true.

Given Condition 1 and Condition 2, A and B are both true. Substitute both into the equation to get:

True AND True = Q

Q = True

Because both A and B are true, then Q must be true. Time to make orange juice!

How a Computer Decides When It Can Make Orange Juice

Condition A (There are oranges in your fridge.)	Condition B (You have an orange squeezer.)	Result Q (You're able to make orange juice.)
False	False	False
False	True	False
True	False	False
True	True	**TRUE!**

MEET THE LOGIC GATES

Many of the circuits inside your computer are physical versions of logic equations, complete with smaller circuits called *logic gates*, which are physical logical operators. A logic gate takes ones and zeros—representing true and false, respectively—as inputs and then outputs a 1 or 0 based on the results of the equation inside.

You can make really awesome projects with logic gates yourself, too!

I remember the first time my dad told me about logic gates: I went straight to my room and spent hours trying to combine them on paper in different ways to add binary numbers. I hope you have as much fun with them as I did! Now, let's look at how a few different logic gates work.

AND Gates Check for Two True Inputs

The *AND gate* is the physical form of the AND operator you used to decide whether you were able to make orange juice. An AND gate has two or more inputs—A and B, for example—and one output—Q, for example. It checks whether A and B are both 1, and if they are, then Q is 1; otherwise, the output is 0. Q is 1 only if both A *and* B are 1; if one or both inputs are 0, the output is 0.

I find it helpful to write out the values of Q that result from different input combinations in a *truth table*. This truth table shows all possible input combinations for the AND gate and what the output will be for each. In a truth table, 0 stands for *false*, and 1 stands for *true*.

AND gate

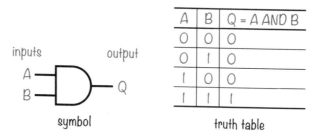

A	B	Q = A AND B
0	0	0
0	1	0
1	0	0
1	1	1

inputs   output

A
B   Q

symbol   truth table

OR Gates Check for One True Input

The *OR gate* checks whether input A *or* input B is 1. If either is 1 or both are 1, then the output Q is also 1. But if both inputs are 0, then the output is 0.

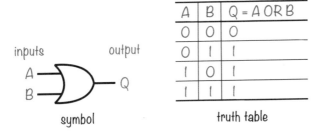

OR gate

A	B	Q = A OR B
0	0	0
0	1	1
1	0	1
1	1	1

symbol   truth table

NOT Gates Flip Inputs

The *NOT gate*, also called an *inverter*, has only one input and
one output, and its function is very simple: the output is the
opposite of the input. If the input is 1, then the output is 0. If
the input is 0, the output is 1.

NOT gate

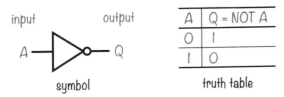

A	Q = NOT A
0	1
1	0

symbol   truth table

A Bigger AND Gate

AND gates and OR gates can have more than two inputs. For
example, here's a 4-input AND gate symbol:

4-input AND gate

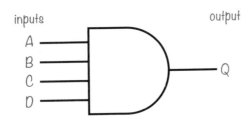

Because it's an AND gate, the result will be 1 only if all four inputs are 1; otherwise, it will be 0. That is, the output Q is true (1) if all four inputs—A, B, C, and D—are true (1):

$$Q = A \text{ AND } B \text{ AND } C \text{ AND } D$$

We can also make a 4-input AND gate from three 2-input AND gates, like this:

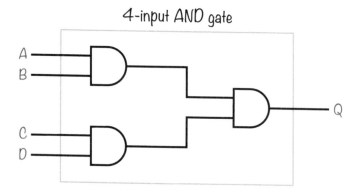

4-input AND gate

HOW TO DRAW LOGIC CIRCUIT DIAGRAMS

You can use logic gates to build a circuit that checks for conditions and decides what to do based on them. For example, imagine you could deactivate your alarm system from Chapter 1 by entering a secret code. Then, you could leave the alarm system on while you're gone, and if someone opened the door, they'd have to know the right code to turn the alarm off. With logic gates, a circuit can check easily whether the right code was entered.

A Logic Equation for a Secret Code

Let's say the secret code is 1001, and when the secret code is detected, an LED should turn on to indicate success. When building logic circuits, it's helpful to write the logic equation for your circuit before building, so let's practice.

First, think about what each 1 and each 0 in the secret code represents in terms of logic gates. In this case, you want the LED to turn on only when four conditions are true, and you can connect those conditions with AND operators as follows.

Let's represent the four bits in the secret code with the letters W, X, Y, and Z. Then, you can check each bit to see whether it's the correct value, testing for $W = 1$, $X = 0$, $Y = 0$, and $Z = 1$.

You'll need to AND the four secret code bits together using a 4-input AND gate. But simply connecting W, X, Y, and Z straight to the AND gate would give this logic equation:

$$Q = W \text{ AND } X \text{ AND } Y \text{ AND } Z$$

This would test whether all the bits are 1 because $Q = 1$ only if W, X, Y, and Z are all 1. Instead, you need to test for the secret code where W and Z are 1, but X and Y are 0.

Fortunately, in Boolean logic, you have only two options: 1 or 0 (true or false). If something is 0, then it is NOT 1; in words, if something is false, then it is NOT true. This means that if $X = 0$ (false), then NOT $X = 1$ (true). Knowing that, you can rewrite the equation as follows:

$$Q = W \text{ AND (NOT } X) \text{ AND (NOT } Y) \text{ AND } Z$$

This equation uses NOT on bits X and Y, which should be 0 for the secret code. The NOT will invert their values, changing 0 to 1 and 1 to 0.

Converting a Logic Equation into a Circuit Diagram

Now we'll draw the secret code equation as a circuit. The final output will be a single 1 or 0. You need a 4-input AND gate to test all four code bits at once, and you're going to make this using three 2-input AND gates as explained earlier. Because you need to test whether the X and Y bits are 0, you'll need to use a NOT gate for each to invert the 0 to 1.

Here's the final circuit:

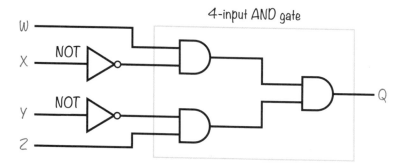

A logic circuit that checks for a secret code (1001)

The first bit (W) should be a 1 and the second (X) should be a 0, so the second bit gets a NOT gate. The third bit (Y) has a NOT gate as well, and it goes into an AND gate with the fourth bit (Z).

The first AND gate should output 1 if it sees W = 1 and X = 0, and the second AND gate should output 1 if it sees Y = 0 and Z = 1. If both of those AND gates output 1, then so will the third AND gate, which ultimately confirms that 1001 was entered.

TRY IT OUT: DRAW MORE LOGICAL STATEMENTS AS CIRCUITS

Now that you've seen the basics, transform a few logical statements of your own into logic circuits on paper. For example, how might you draw up plans for a "Can I Make Orange Juice?" decision maker? Create one based on the statements under "It's Only Logical" on page 214.

USING LOGIC GATES IN REAL LIFE

When I learned about logic gates, I thought they'd be small two- and three-legged components. But logic gates come boxed inside integrated circuits (ICs). Each IC contains several gates, so even if you want to use just one, you'll have to use an IC anyway.

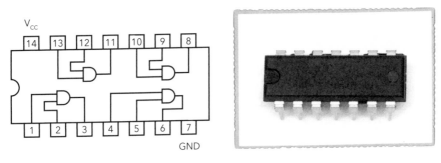

It's also important to know that logic gate outputs don't supply much current. Even if a logic gate outputs 5 V, that doesn't mean that you can connect your 5 V motor to it. The logic gate simply can't give enough current for the motor to run.

Recall from Chapter 7 that a transistor needs only a little current flowing into its base to turn on and let a lot more current flow from its collector to emitter. When you want to use a logic gate to turn on a circuit or component that requires more current, you can connect the logic gate to a transistor. Do you remember the circuit from "Project #14: Build a Circuit that Senses Touch" on page 136? You can modify this circuit to turn on an LED from a logic gate, like this:

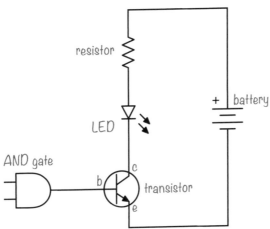

I'll show you how to incorporate this into a project in the next section.

MORE ABOUT CURRENT, COMPONENTS, AND TRANSISTORS

You can easily replace the LED and resistor with something else that you want to control, like a motor, a fan, or a relay. But when doing this, be mindful of the current. How much current does your motor need, and how much current can the transistor handle?

Both values can be found in the components' datasheets. For transistors, the value you are looking for is called I_C, or *collector current*. According to the datasheet of a BC547 transistor, its maximum collector current is 100 mA. That's more than enough to power an LED, which usually uses about 15 to 20 mA at the most.

But what if you want to connect a motor? First, you'd need to find out how much current the motor needs, and you'll find that in the motor's datasheet. If a motor needs 500 mA, you'll need to connect it to a transistor that can handle more than 500 mA of current. For example, a PN2222 transistor can handle up to 600 mA, so it should be able to switch the motor on and off.

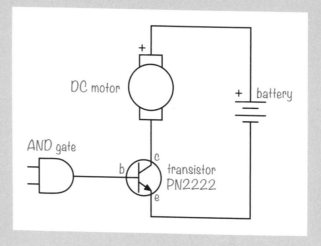

PROJECT #21: A SECRET CODE CHECKER

In this project, you'll build a logic circuit that checks whether a set of four input bits matches a secret code. You'll use four switches, inside one DIP switch, to set the code. If the input bits match the code, then the logic circuit should output a voltage, representing a 1; otherwise, it should output zero voltage, to indicate 0. This final output will go to a transistor so you can use it to control something—like an alarm!

The basic Secret Code Checker circuit turns on an LED when you input the right code. At the end of the project, I'll show you how to use the Secret Code Checker to disarm your intruder alarm from Chapter 1.

Here's the complete circuit diagram for this project:

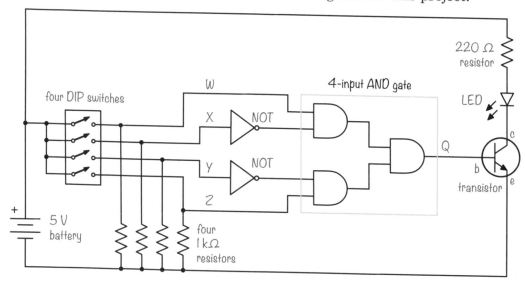

Shopping List

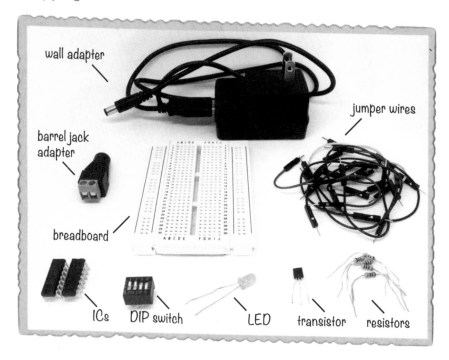

▶ **A breadboard** (Jameco #20601, Bitsbox #CN329) with at least 30 rows.

- **Breadboard jumper wires** (Jameco #2237044, Bitsbox #CN236)—you'll need around 20 for this project.
- **A DIP switch** (Jameco #38820, Bitsbox #SW042) with four individual switches.
- **A 74LS04 inverter IC with six NOT gates** (Jameco #46316, Bitsbox #QU108)
- **A 74LS08 IC with four AND gates** (Jameco #46375, Bitsbox #QU109)
- **A general-purpose NPN transistor** (Jameco #254801, Bitsbox #QD011), such as BC547.
- **A standard LED** (Jameco #34761, Bitsbox #OP003)
- **A 220 Ω resistor** (Jameco #690700, Bitsbox #CR25220R) to limit the current to the LED.
- **Four 1 kΩ resistors** (Jameco #690865, Bitsbox #CR251K) to use as pull-down resistors.
- **A 5 V DC wall adapter** (Jameco #2126125, Bitsbox #TF010) to power the circuit.
- **A DC barrel jack adapter** (Jameco #2227209, Bitsbox #CN424) to connect the wall adapter to the breadboard.

Tools

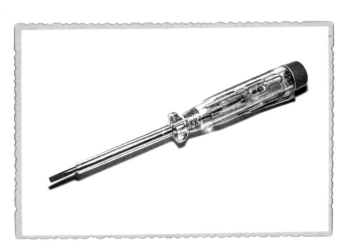

- **A screwdriver** that fits the screw terminal of the barrel jack adapter.

How to Use Other Voltages with a Breadboard

You've used 9 V batteries for each circuit in this book so far, but most digital circuits need to use lower voltages. For example, a lot of ICs with logic gates inside use 5 V instead. But 5 V is not a standard battery value; there are 4.5 V and 6 V batteries, but not 5 V.

What can you do when your circuit requires 5 V? Say hello to the *wall adapter* and the *barrel jack adapter*.

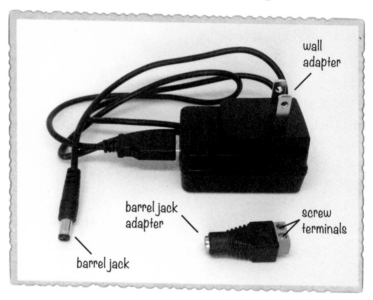

Many electronic devices use wall adapters to recharge batteries or just to stay powered. The pronged side of a wall adapter plugs into a wall socket, and the other side plugs into something you want to power. Wall adapters come in many values, and this project uses a 5 V DC regulated adapter.

To supply power to a circuit, the wall adapter in this project needs to plug into a barrel jack adapter. The barrel jack adapter listed in this project's Shopping List (page 224) has two *screw terminals*, where you can plug in jumper wires that connect to the breadboard. You can connect any wall adapter with the standard round plug into this barrel jack adapter.

MAKING CIRCUITS MORE RELIABLE

If a circuit needs an input voltage and you don't connect the input to anything, then that input is *floating*. A floating input is unreliable because the circuit may see it as a 1 or a 0, and you can't control which.

The individual switches on a DIP switch are either open or closed. When the switch is open, the input it controls will be floating if it's not connected to anything else. To fix this, you can attach a *pull-down resistor* to each input on the logic gates, like this:

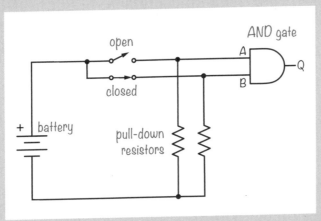

Each pull-down resistor in this circuit diagram connects to a switch and a gate input on one side and to the negative battery terminal on the other. When a switch is open, the resistor "pulls" the gate input down to 0 V, which is a 0. When a switch is closed, the gate input connects to the positive terminal and gets the positive supply voltage, which is a 1.

In this project's circuit diagram on page 224, there are four switches with 1 kΩ pull-down resistors. All of them are shown as open, and all of the AND gate inputs would be 0 in that state.

Step 1: Place the Switches and Resistors

Plug your DIP switch in at the top of the breadboard, with one side of the switch on each side of the notch in the middle. Use jumper wires to connect the left side of each DIP switch to the positive supply rail on the left, and connect a 1 kΩ resistor from the right side of each DIP switch to the negative supply rail on the right.

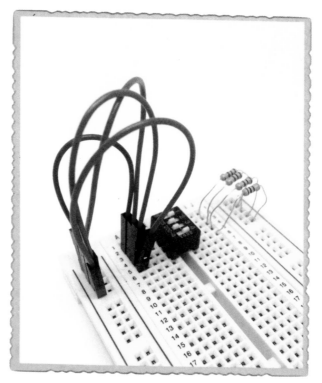

Step 2: Place the ICs

Place the IC with NOT gates, marked *74LS04*, in the middle of the breadboard and place the IC with AND gates, marked *74LS08*, farther down. For both ICs, point the rounded notch toward the DIP switch. Leave at least three rows at the bottom of the breadboard for the transistor.

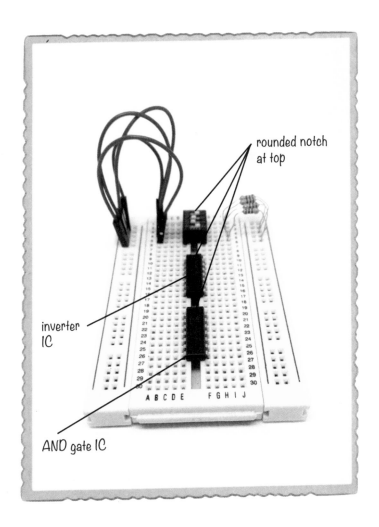

rounded notch
at top

inverter
IC

AND gate IC

A B C D E   F G H I J

Step 3: Place the Transistor and LED

Plug your transistor into three rows at the bottom of the breadboard. If you used the BC547 transistor from this project's
Shopping List (page 224), face the flat side left so that the
collector is the upper pin, the base is the middle pin, and the
emitter is the bottom pin. If you used a different NPN transistor, check its datasheet to see which pin is which.

Connect the LED's short leg, the cathode, to the same
row as the collector. Connect the LED's long leg, the anode, to
an empty row on the left side of the breadboard. Finally, connect the 220 Ω resistor from the LED's anode to the positive
supply rail.

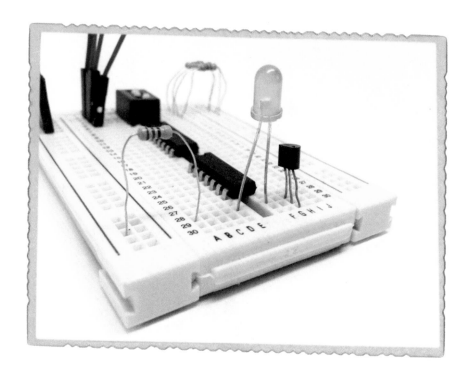

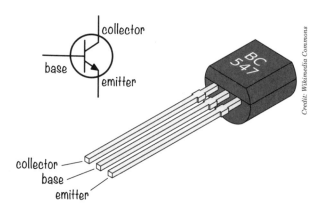

Credit: Wikimedia Commons

Step 4: Build the Logic Circuit

First, look at the following diagram to see where the AND and NOT gates are inside your ICs and to see the connections you need to make.

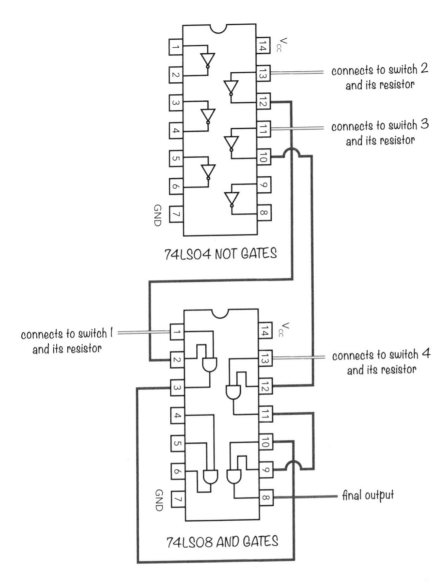

connects to switch 2
and its resistor

connects to switch 3
and its resistor

74LS04 NOT GATES

connects to switch 1
and its resistor

connects to switch 4
and its resistor

final output

74LS08 AND GATES

Take four jumper wires and connect them from the switch outputs to the gate inputs as follows:

▶ The output from switch 1, the uppermost switch, goes to the AND gate input on pin 1 of the lower IC (74LS08).

▶ The switch 2 output goes to the NOT gate input on pin 13 on the upper IC (74LS04).

▶ The switch 3 output goes to the NOT gate input on pin 11 on the upper IC.

▶ The switch 4 output goes to the AND gate input on pin 13 of the lower IC.

Next, get two jumper wires to connect the outputs of the NOT gates to the AND gate inputs like this:

▶ One jumper wire goes from pin 12 on the upper IC to pin 2 on the lower IC.

▶ The other jumper wire goes from pin 10 on the upper IC to pin 12 on the lower IC.

Now, each output from the AND gates needs to go into the third AND gate, as follows:

▶ Connect one jumper wire from pin 3 to pin 10 of the lower IC.

▶ Connect another jumper wire from pin 11 to pin 9 on the lower IC.

▶ Finally, connect a jumper wire from the final output of the AND gate with the other side hanging loose for now.

Your IC connections should look like this:

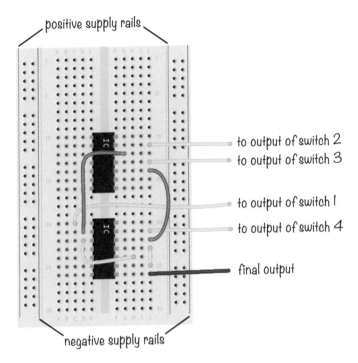

positive supply rails

to output of switch 2
to output of switch 3

to output of switch 1
to output of switch 4

final output

negative supply rails

Step 5: Finish Wiring the Transistor

Now, connect the output from the final AND gate—pin 8 of
the lower IC—to the base of the transistor. This output will
control whether the transistor allows current to pass through
to the LED or not. Connect a jumper wire from the emitter of
the transistor to the negative supply rail.

PROTECTING YOUR COMPONENTS

The circuit for this project relies on the fact that gates supply only a tiny amount of current to the transistor base. Your transistor will be perfectly fine while you use your secret code checker, but to protect the transistor base from damage by larger currents in other circuits, you should place a resistor around 1 to 10 kΩ between the transistor base and its current source—in this case, the AND gate output.

Transistors also should usually be protected in motor circuits, like the one in "More About Current, Components, and Transistors" on page 222. That circuit should work as is, but to be really careful, it's good to connect a diode across the motor, with the cathode on the positive side. That should protect the transistor from any high-voltage spikes that might happen when the motor is switched off.

Step 6: Power and Test the Secret Code Checker

Connect jumper wires from pin 14 on both ICs to the positive supply rail and from pin 7 of both chips to the negative supply rail. Then, turn off all the switches on the DIP switch and connect your 5 V source, with plus to the positive supply on the left and minus to the negative supply on the right.

Use your barrel jack adapter with a couple of jumper wires to make this connection. The barrel jack adapter should have + and – markings to tell you which supply is which. Just loosen the screws on the adapter, insert a wire into each, and tighten the screws again. Follow the conventional color code by using a red wire for positive and a black wire for negative so you will be sure to connect them the correct way on your breadboard.

The LED should stay dark when the switches are off, but when you set the code to 1001 by switching on the top and bottom switches, it should light up.

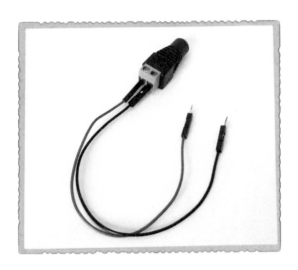

Step 7: What If the LED Doesn't Light Up?

First, check that the two ICs have power. Do both ICs have pin 14 connected to the positive supply column and pin 7 connected to the negative supply column? If you find the ICs become too hot to touch, disconnect the 5 V power supply from the wall immediately and wait for the ICs to cool down. Then, make certain you have the supply connections the correct way before trying again. The wire plugged into the barrel jack adapter's positive (+) terminal should be plugged into the positive supply column on the breadboard, and the wire in the barrel jack adapter's negative (–) terminal should be plugged into the negative supply column.

If the ICs are powered and the circuit still doesn't work, then check the input values on the switches. Use a multimeter to measure the voltage from the negative supply rail to the pins on the AND and NOT gates that take inputs from the switches. You should get 5 V on pins 1 and 13 of the AND IC and 0 V on pins 11 and 13 of the NOT IC. Check that the output from each AND gate you're using is 5 V, too; you should see 5 V on pins 3, 8, and 11. If any AND gate in the IC doesn't output 5 V, then one of its inputs is 0 V. Figure out why it's 0 V, and you should find the problem.

TRY IT OUT:
DISARM YOUR INTRUDER ALARM

Instead of an LED and a resistor, you can connect a relay to the Secret Code Checker and combine this project with the intruder alarm you built in Chapter 1. Connect the 9 V battery to the intruder alarm through the relay so that when you input the right code, the power to the alarm is cut and the noise stops. Refer back to "Meet the Relay" on page 97 to see how to connect a relay.

Notice that the secret code checker, with its 5 V supply, is being used to control the completely separate intruder alarm circuit with a 9 V supply. Connecting two circuits with separate power supplies this way is okay because there's no electrical connection between the two circuits. Relays are useful when you need to control a circuit with a different type of power supply!

Here's the circuit:

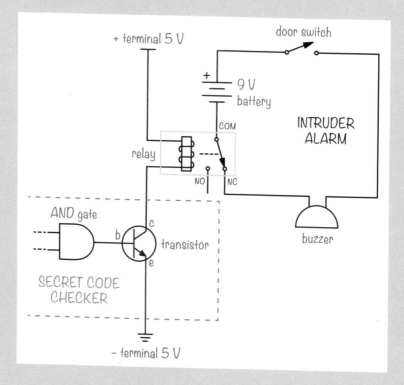

And these are the components you'll need:

▶ **The circuit from "Project #2: Intruder Alarm" on page 11**

▶ **The circuit from "Project #21: A Secret Code Checker" on page 223**

▶ **A 5 V relay** (Jameco #842996, Bitsbox #SW073)

NEGATIVE LOGIC GATES

AND, OR, and NOT are basic logic gates, and you can combine them to create new ones. Let's look at two more gates that are created this way.

NAND Looks for One False Input

The *NAND gate* works like an AND gate with a NOT gate inverter on the output. The little circle on the output means NOT. That means the output from the NAND gate is 0 when both A and B are 1.

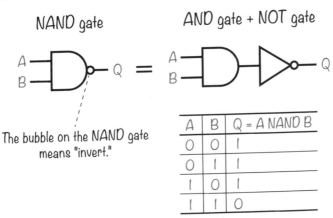

NAND gate

AND gate + NOT gate

A
B — Q = A
B — Q

The bubble on the NAND gate means "invert."

A	B	Q = A NAND B
0	0	1
0	1	1
1	0	1
1	1	0

NOR Looks for Two False Inputs

The *NOR gate* works like an OR gate with an inverter on the output. The output is 1 when both A and B are 0.

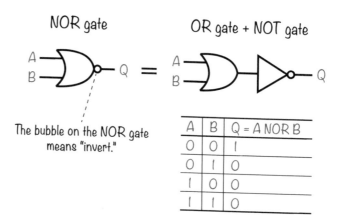

NOR gate

OR gate + NOT gate

A
B ⟩—○ Q = A
B ⟩—▷—○ Q

The bubble on the NOR gate means "invert."

A	B	Q = A NOR B
0	0	1
0	1	0
1	0	0
1	1	0

WHAT'S NEXT?

In this chapter, you learned how to use logic gates to build circuits that "decide" things, like whether a code is correct or not. And at the end, you got to see some negative logic gates as well. Understanding how negative logic gates work is helpful, because they are often used in real-life circuits. In fact, you'll use them in Chapter 11.

If you want to explore gates a bit further, I suggest you try combining some logic gates you've learned about on paper to create an *XOR gate*. An XOR gate gives out 1 only if the inputs are different from each other.

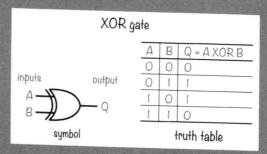

XOR gate

inputs   output

A
B ⟩⟩— Q

symbol

A	B	Q = A XOR B
0	0	0
0	1	1
1	0	1
1	1	0

truth table

By combining logic gates in different ways, you can create almost anything you can imagine. But that might be a bit hard to see right now, so in the next chapter, I'm going to show you some more building blocks you can create with logic gates. You'll learn how to build your own memory circuit, and then you'll build your own electronic coin tosser!

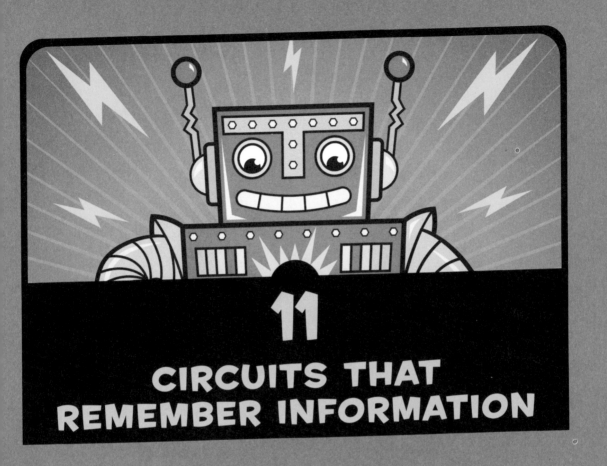

CIRCUITS THAT REMEMBER INFORMATION

n Chapter 9, you learned how to store bits using switches. As long as the switches don't change, the bits stay the same. But you have to manually set the switches, and that's not very efficient. In Chapter 10, you learned about logic gates and how you can use them to play with ones and zeroes. Now, I'll show you how to use logic gates to make electronic memory that saves bits, even after you change the input. At the end of this chapter, you'll build your own electronic coin tosser!

SAVING ONE BIT AT A TIME

One simple memory circuit is an *SR latch*. You can create an SR latch with two NOR gates, and one latch can store one bit of data.

SR latch

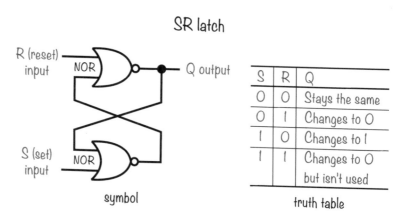

S	R	Q
0	0	Stays the same
0	1	Changes to 0
1	0	Changes to 1
1	1	Changes to 0 but isn't used

symbol   truth table

Q starts at 0, and this circuit won't update its output until you use R or S to tell it to, which is called *latching* the bit. S and R stand for *set* and *reset*, respectively: when you set the latch, Q changes to 1. When you reset it, Q changes to 0. As the SR latch truth table describes, you can set the latch by putting a 1 on the S input and a 0 on the R input. To reset it, you'd put a 1 on the R input and a 0 on the S input. Let's look at how setting Q to 1 works.

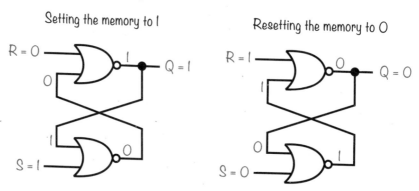

Setting the memory to 1   Resetting the memory to 0

The output from a NOR gate is 1 when all inputs are 0. When S (set) is 1, the output of the lower NOR gate is 0, no matter what that gate's other input is. The output is connected to an input on the other NOR gate, together with R (reset). Because R is 0, you have two 0s into the upper NOR gate, which makes Q output 1.

A BETTER MEMORY CIRCUIT

If you add a few more gates to the SR latch, you can create a *D latch*, which sets the output Q to whatever the D input is when the C input is 1.

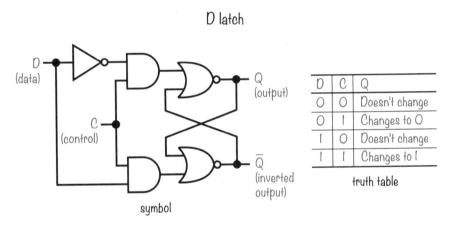

D latch

D	C	Q
O	O	Doesn't change
O	1	Changes to O
1	O	Doesn't change
1	1	Changes to 1

truth table

The D latch is an improvement over the SR latch because you can change D, the *data input*, as much as you want, and Q won't change unless you set C, the *control input*, to 1. The lower NOR gate output will always be the opposite of the output Q, and that output is labeled $\bar{Q}$ to show this.

MEMORY THAT CHANGES ONLY AT A CERTAIN TIME

The D latch has one weakness: when C is 1, changing D also changes the output Q. What if you don't want the output to change immediately?

Computers use a *clock signal* to tell the circuits inside when something should happen, like when to store new data from a wire. A clock signal is just a voltage that turns on and off continuously—that is, it keeps switching between 1 and 0. This signal is similar to the one you sent to the speaker in "Project #16: Make Your Own Sound with the 555 Timer" on page 167.

To reduce the chance of errors, actions like calculations or storing data happen only when the clock signal switches from off to on or from on to off. This is called *edge-triggering*. If a circuit does something when the clock signal changes from off to on, then that action happens on the rising edge, and the circuit is *positive edge-triggered*. A circuit that triggers an action on the falling edge, when the clock changes from on to off, is *negative edge-triggered*.

A *flip-flop* is a latch that updates its output when triggered by the edge of a clock signal, and you can create one by combining two D latches and a NOT gate. This is called a *D flip-flop*.

D flip-flop

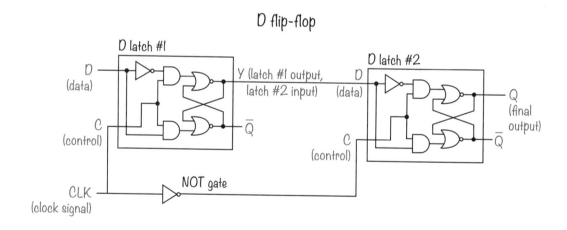

The output voltage Q can change only when the CLK voltage changes from high to low, from 1 to 0. Here's how that works.

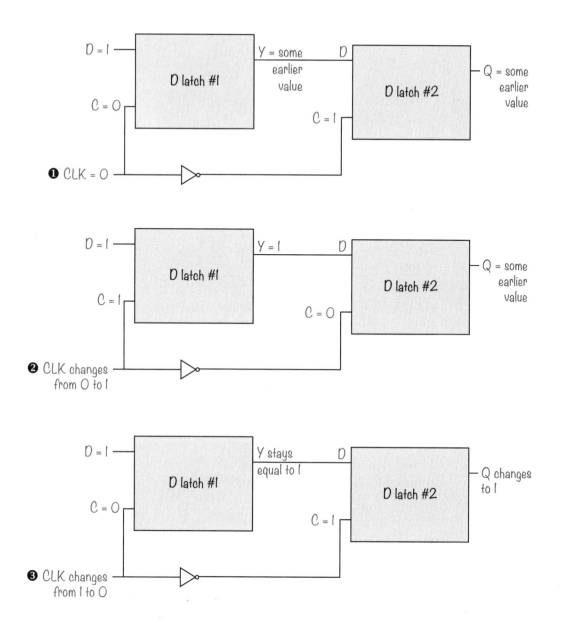

When CLK is 0, Y and Q don't change ❶. When CLK changes to 1 ❷, Y changes to match the D input to D latch #1. But the NOT gate inverts the 1, setting C on D latch #2 to 0 so Q doesn't change. As CLK goes back to 0 ❸, C on D latch #2 changes to 1, the value on Y is saved in latch #2, and Q changes to match Y.

NOTE *Q updates when the clock signal changes from high to low voltage, so this flip-flop is negative edge-triggered.*

This is the circuit diagram symbol for a positive edge-triggered D flip-flop:

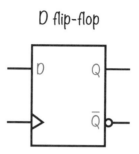

D flip-flop

Instead of writing CLK for the clock input, the D flip-flop symbol has a > marking. Notice the bubble on the $\bar{Q}$ output. Just like on the NOT gate symbol, the bubble means $\bar{Q}$ is the inverted version of Q.

AN OUTPUT THAT TOGGLES

With a simple wire, you can turn a D flip-flop into a circuit that toggles another circuit on and off. For example, imagine you want to turn a light on and off. The D flip-flop stores a value on its input, D, when its clock goes from low to high voltage (if positive edge-triggered). If you connect the D flip-flop's inverted output $\bar{Q}$ to D, the flip-flop's input will always be the opposite of Q. Every time the clock input triggers, the output will change to the opposite value, and the light will toggle.

We start with these values:

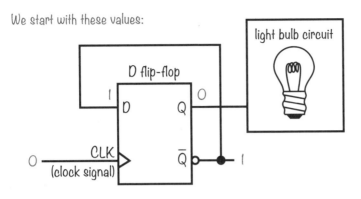

When the clock input changes from 0 to 1, the values are toggled:

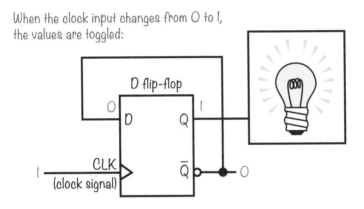

Let's see this concept in action!

PROJECT #22: AN ELECTRONIC COIN TOSSER

For this project, you'll build an electronic coin tosser with a 555 timer, a D flip-flop, a push button, and two LEDs.

In Chapter 8, you built several 555 timer circuits that switched voltages on and off. A circuit that turns a voltage on and off continuously is called an *oscillator*, and in this project, you're going to use an oscillator circuit as an input to the toggling D flip-flop. Do you recognize the oscillator circuit in this diagram?

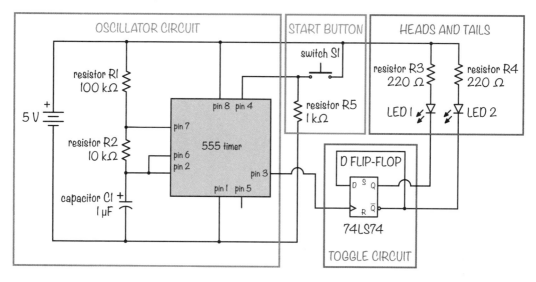

The 555 timer oscillator circuit creates a clock signal that goes to the D flip-flop, causing the output to switch on and off, or *toggle*, continuously as long as you press a push button. The changing output from the D flip-flop turns the LEDs on and off.

When you let go of the push button, the clock signal from the 555 timer stops. The flip-flop output will stop alternating, and only one of the two LEDs will be on: one for heads or the other for tails.

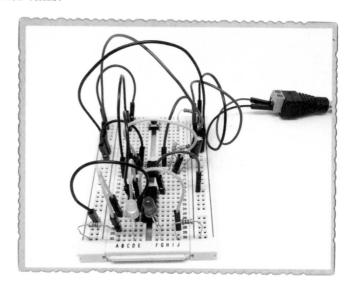

Shopping List

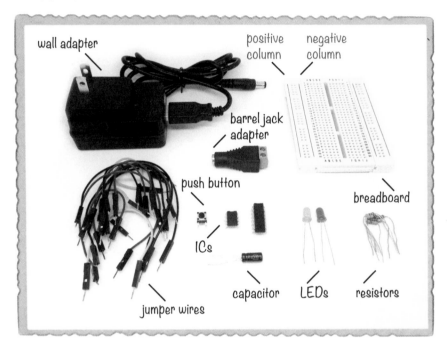

▶ **A breadboard** (Jameco #20601, Bitsbox #CN329) with at least 30 rows.

▶ **Breadboard jumper wires** (Jameco #2237044, Bitsbox #CN236)—you'll need around 20 for this project.

▶ **A 555 timer IC** (Jameco #904085, Bitsbox #QU001) to create the input signal to be counted.

▶ **An IC with two D flip-flops** (Jameco #48004, Bitsbox #QU193)

▶ **A standard green LED** (Jameco #34761, Bitsbox #OP003)

▶ **A standard red LED** (Jameco #333973, Bitsbox #OP002)

▶ **Two 220 Ω resistors** (Jameco #690700, Bitsbox #CR25220R) for limiting the current to the LEDs.

- **A 100 kΩ resistor** (Jameco #691340, Bitsbox #CR25100K) to help set the frequency of the sound.
- **A 10 kΩ resistor** (Jameco #691104, Bitsbox #CR2510K) to help set the frequency of the sound.
- **A 1 kΩ resistor** (Jameco #690865, Bitsbox #CR251K) to use as a pull-down resistor for the start button.
- **A 1 µF capacitor** (Jameco #29831, Bitsbox #EC1U063) to help set the frequency of the sound.
- **A push button** (Jameco #119011, Bitsbox #SW087) to "toss the coin."
- **A 5 V DC wall adapter** (Jameco #2126125, Bitsbox #TF010) to power the circuit.
- **A DC barrel jack adapter** (Jameco #2227209, Bitsbox #CN424) to connect the wall adapter to the breadboard.

This circuit uses the positive and negative supply columns on both sides of the breadboard. When I say to connect a component to the negative or positive supply column "on the left," that means you should use one of the supply columns on the left side of the breadboard. On both sides, the positive column is marked with a red line to the left, and the negative is marked with a blue line to the right.

Step 1: Build the Oscillator Circuit

First, let's wire up the 555 timer:

1. Plug the 555 timer into the breadboard near the middle.
2. Connect R1, the 100 kΩ resistor, from pin 7 of the 555 timer to the positive supply column on the right.
3. Connect R2, the 10 kΩ resistor, from pin 6 to pin 7.
4. Connect C1, the 1 µF capacitor, from pin 6 to the negative supply column on the right. If you're using a polarized capacitor like the one I suggest in the Shopping List, make

sure you connect the negative leg to the negative supply column. The negative leg should be marked with a minus or a zero on the capacitor itself.

5. Connect a jumper wire from pin 2 to pin 6 of the 555 timer.

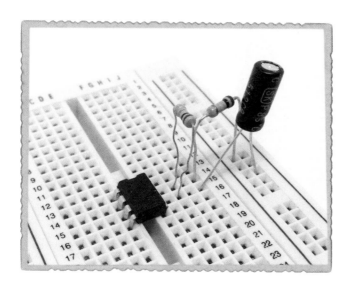

Step 2: Add the Start Button

Now, connect the push button between pin 4 on the 555 timer and the positive supply column as follows:

1. Place the push button at the very top of the breadboard, across the notch in the middle. By connecting it like this, you should have one side of the switch on the top row and the other side on row 3.

2. Connect a wire from pin 4 of the 555 timer to the lower pins of the push button (row 3). Connect a wire from the upper pins of the push button (row 1) to the positive supply column on the left.

3.   Connect R5, the 1 kΩ pull-down resistor, from the lower pins of the push button to the negative supply column on the right.

The 555 timer also needs to be powered. Connect a jumper wire from pin 1 to the negative supply column on the left. Use another jumper wire to connect pin 8 to the positive supply column on the right.

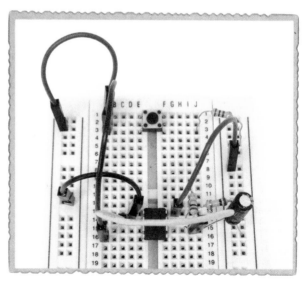

Step 3: Build the Toggle Circuit

Place the IC with the D flip-flops—marked *74LS74*—below the 555 timer so that it straddles the notch in the breadboard, with the notch pointing to the top of the breadboard. This IC contains two D flip-flops, but you'll use only the D flip-flop on pins 1 to 6.

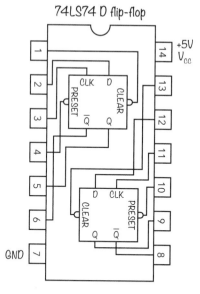

74LS74 D flip-flop

Run a jumper wire from the inverted output $\overline{Q}$ on pin 6 of the 74LS74 D flip-flop to the D-input at pin 2. Connect the output from pin 3 on the 555 timer to pin 3 on the D flip-flop, which is the clock input.

The D flip-flop needs power, too. Connect pin 14 to the positive supply column on the right and connect pin 7 to the negative supply column on the left.

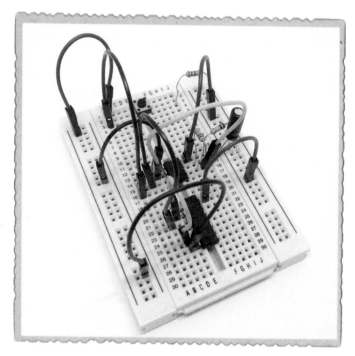

Step 4: Add the Heads and Tails LEDs

In the previous project, you used a transistor to power an LED from a logic gate output because the gate couldn't provide enough current. This circuit has the same challenge because D flip-flops are just a few logic gates in an IC, but there's a little trick you can use to get around that limitation.

The 74LS74 D flip-flop's datasheet says this IC will allow only about 0.5 mA to flow when the output voltage is high, but it allows 8 mA when the output voltage is low. (Search online for *74LS74 datasheet* if you're curious to read the datasheet for yourself.) If you connect the LEDs and resistors to the positive supply column on one side and to the flip-flop output on the other, the LEDs should get 8 mA of current when the output is low, turning them on. It may seem strange to connect the LEDs like this, instead of connecting them to the negative supply column, but doing so makes the LEDs light when the output from the gate is 0 instead of 1.

Whatever value Q has, $\bar{Q}$ will always be the opposite. If you connect an LED to each output, one will light up and the other won't. Add the heads and tails LEDs as follows:

1. Plug the two LEDs into the bottom of the breadboard, with the red LED on the right side of the middle notch and the green LED on the left side. Place the longer leads (the anodes) in the bottom row and the shorter leads (the cathodes) a couple of rows above.

2. Connect one jumper wire from pin 5 of the D flip-flop to the short leg of the red LED. Then connect another jumper wire from pin 6 of the D flip-flop to the short leg of the green LED.

3. Connect a resistor from each bottom row to the positive supply column on each side (R3 and R4 from the circuit diagram).

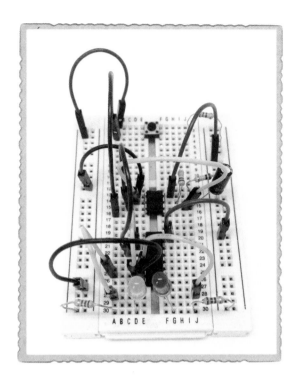

Step 5: Toss that "Coin"!

Use a jumper wire to connect the left negative supply column to the one on the right, and do the same for the two positive supply columns. Then, connect two jumper wires to your barrel jack adapter—connect the plus side to one of the positive supply columns and connect the minus side to one of the negative supply columns.

Finally, plug the wall adapter into the barrel jack adapter first and then into the wall socket. One LED should light up right away. When you push the button, the LEDs should alternate quickly between on and off. Release the button, and only one should be lit.

Now, you can use this circuit to make decisions. For example, say you ask yourself, "Should I go out and play football this weekend, or should I play baseball?" Green means go out and play football; red means baseball. Or, if you're arguing with one of your friends about who gets the last cookie, then let the coin tosser decide!

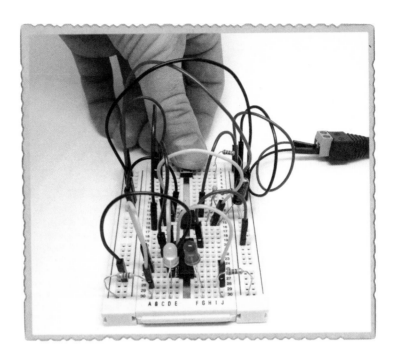

Step 6: What If the Coin Tosser Doesn't Work?

First, check that you're using a 5 V wall adapter. Any other voltages might not work.

Then, if one LED is lit but nothing happens when you push the button, check that the D flip-flop is connected correctly. If no LEDs are lit, there's definitely something wrong with the D flip-flop and LED parts of the circuit. Carefully compare your connections with the circuit diagram at the beginning of this project. If your circuit isn't working after you know the LED and flip-flop circuits are connected correctly, then check the 555 timer connections.

To help you avoid the same mistakes, I'll share the problems I had when building this for the first time:

▶ I connected the LEDs to pins 4 and 5 of the D flip-flop instead of pins 5 and 6.

▶ I connected the capacitor to pin 5 of the 555 timer instead of pin 6.

▶ I forgot to connect the positive supply column on the left to the one on the right.

WHAT'S NEXT?

You've built a lot of different circuits in this book! At this point you have a solid foundation in electronics, both in theory and practical experience. Now, the next step is to focus on what you think is fun. Find a project you really want to build—and go make it!

The best way to continue learning is to build lots of circuits and read about anything you're curious about. Follow tutorials online and find more books on different topics in electronics.

In Chapter 12, the final chapter, I'll show you how to build one last project: a really cool game where you have to test your reaction speed by "catching" a light. After that, I hope you'll continue exploring, playing, and having fun with electronics. There are so many great things you can build!

12

LET'S MAKE A GAME!

Y ou've built all sorts of small circuits in this book, and each circuit was designed to teach you a particular concept. In this chapter, you'll combine all your new skills to build a reaction game. The game has a row of five LEDs that light up one at a time so that a light appears to run back and forth.

The goal of the game is to stop the light when it's in the middle of the five LEDs. That gives you 10 points. If you stop it on an LED next to the middle one, you get 5 points. But if you stop it on one of the end LEDs, you lose all your points and have to start over from 0. Try to reach 50 points!

You can play this game by yourself to practice your reaction time, or with as many friends as you want. If you're competing with friends, I suggest giving each player only one attempt at stopping the light before the next player gets a turn.

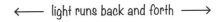

← light runs back and forth →

If you stop on the green light, you get 10 points!

If you stop on a blue light, you get 5 points!

If you stop on a red light, you lose all your points!

MEET THE REACTION GAME CIRCUITS

The reaction game will consist of three circuits:

▶ A 555 timer circuit that determines the speed of the game

▶ A counter that controls which LED light to turn on

▶ An SR latch that will add a reset button and an action button

This section explains each circuit, but to help you understand their diagrams, let's meet two new circuit symbols.

Meet the V_{CC} and GND Symbols

Circuit diagrams don't always use a battery symbol like the one used throughout this book. Sometimes they use the V_{CC} (or V_{DD}) and *GND* symbols instead.

V_{cc} symbol   GND symbol

If nothing in the circuit diagram or its description says otherwise, you can assume that V_{CC} represents the positive side of the battery and that GND represents the negative side, or ground. The symbols sometimes look a little different, but the V_{CC} symbol usually shows a wire connecting down from its symbol to the circuit, while the GND symbol shows a wire connecting up from the symbol to the circuit.

In bigger circuit diagrams, like the one you're going to build from in this chapter, these symbols make the diagram much easier to draw and understand.

WHY IS IT CALLED V_{cc}?

The positive voltage symbol is called V_{CC} because of old naming conventions. V_{CC} was the voltage supplied to the collector side of a transistor in common transistor circuits, usually through a resistor or some other components. The collector is where the "CC" comes from.

You've used a bipolar junction transistor throughout this book, but there's another type of transistor called a *field-effect transistor (FET)*. The pin that equals the collector on this type of transistor is called the *drain*, so the voltage that was supplied to the drain side of the FET was called V_{DD}.

A 555 Timer to Set the Light Speed

The circuit that sets the reaction game's speed will be built around a 555 timer, and it's similar to the circuits you built in Chapter 8. The components in this circuit diagram will set the game to a "medium" speed: it's not super fast, and it's not super slow.

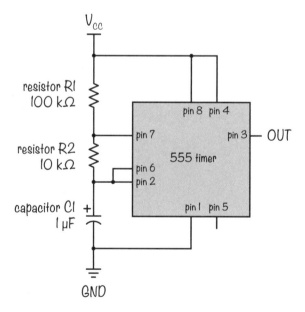

Every time the output from the 555 timer goes from low to high, the light moves one step to the side. The number of times the output from the 555 timer goes high per second is the frequency of the output. As I showed in Chapter 8, the formula for calculating the frequency of the output of the 555 timer is

$$\text{Frequency} = \frac{1.44}{(R1 + R2 + R2) \times C1}$$

The following values from the 555 timer circuit diagram correspond to that formula:

$$R1 = 100 \text{ k}\Omega$$

$$R2 = 10 \text{ k}\Omega$$

$$C1 = 1 \text{ }\mu F$$

Plug these into the formula, keeping in mind that 1 µF = 0.000001 F and 120 kΩ = 120,000 Ω, and you get this:

$$\text{Frequency} = \frac{1.44}{(100 \text{ k}\Omega + 10 \text{ k}\Omega + 10 \text{ k}\Omega) \times 1 \text{ }\mu F}$$

$$\text{Frequency} = \frac{1.44}{120 \text{ k}\Omega \times 1 \text{ }\mu F}$$

$$\text{Frequency} = \frac{1.44}{120{,}000 \text{ }\Omega \times 0.000001 \text{ F}}$$

$$\text{Frequency} = 12 \text{ Hz}$$

This means the output will go high 12 times per second and the light will change places 12 times per second. You can experiment with the component values for R1, R2, and C1 later to speed up or slow down the game.

A Counter to Turn the LEDs On

To control the LEDs, you'll use a *decade counter*, which is an IC that counts input pulses. Every time the clock input on pin 14 goes from low to high, the counter increments by one. It counts from 0 to 9, and it has 10 outputs marked 0 to 9.

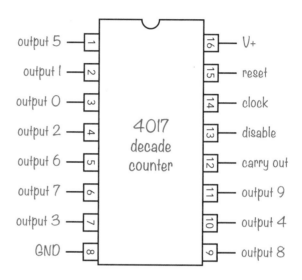

For example, when the counter has counted three input pulses, output 3 (that is, pin 7) is high, and the other pins are low. If you connect an LED to output 3, then when the counter is at three, the LED will turn on.

If you connect LEDs to several output pins, then as the counter increases, the LEDs turn on in order, according to their output pins. When the counter is at 9 and receives a 10th input pulse, it goes back to 0 and turns the output pins on in order again.

But the counter counts pulses only if pin 13 is low. This means you can use pin 13 to tell the game when to start moving the light across the LEDs and when to stop the light.

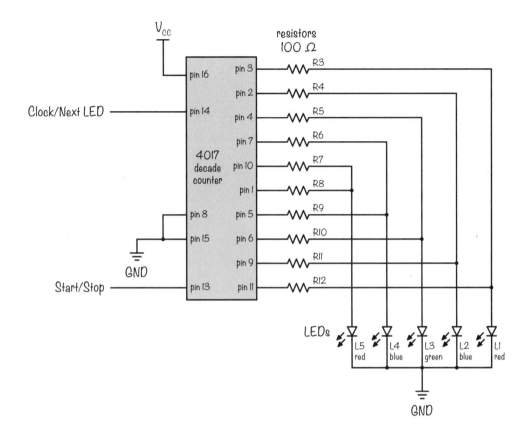

Each output has a resistor to reduce the current through the LED and make sure the LED doesn't get destroyed. Because two output pins connect to each LED, the resistors keep the voltage to each LED high, even though one output will be low and one will be high. The resistors also ensure that two outputs aren't connected directly together, which could damage the IC when one output is high and the other low.

A Latch to Start and Stop the Light

Do you remember the SR latch from "Saving One Bit at a Time" on page 240? The start/stop circuit for this game is a similar SR latch but built with two NAND gates. (The SR latch in Chapter 11 used NOR gates.)

The SR latch is a circuit that can remember a single bit. Its output is either 0 or 1, and it keeps that number until it gets set or reset with a new input.

You can create a circuit that tells the latch what to output with two buttons: one for setting the output to 1 and one for setting the output to 0. Using NAND gates instead of NOR gates means the buttons must make the inputs low to output a 1.

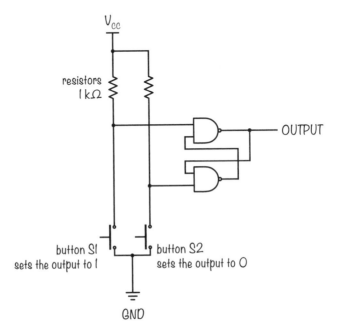

In this circuit, it doesn't matter whether you click the buttons quickly or slowly. The 1-button always sets the output to 1, and the 0-button always sets the output to 0.

That's perfect for the reaction game! Connecting the output to the start/stop pin, or pin 13, on the decade counter gives you a button for starting and stopping the LEDs.

PROJECT #23: AN LED REACTION GAME

It's time to put all the pieces I showed you together to build the reaction game. This circuit has a lot of connections, but I know you can make it. Just don't rush. Take your time and test each part of the circuit after the step where I explain how to build it.

I also recommend using a bigger breadboard than you've used in the previous projects, because this circuit is huge!

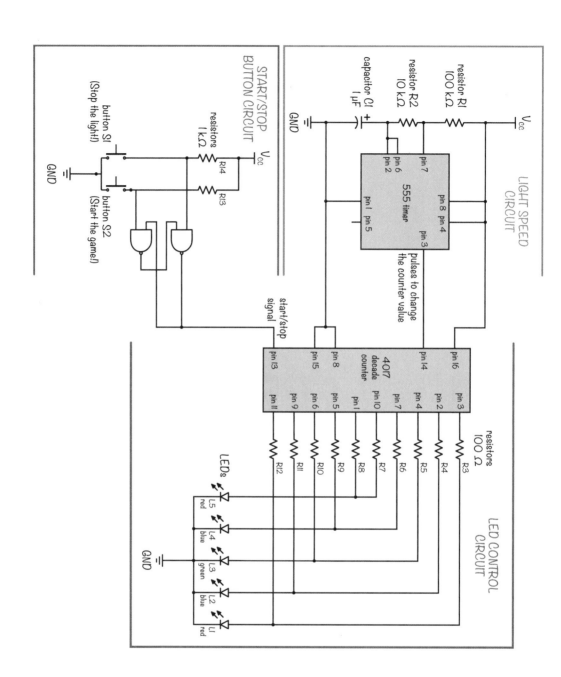

START/STOP
BUTTON CIRCUIT

button S1
(Stop the light!)

resistors
1 kΩ

V_{cc}

R14

R13

button S2
(Start the game!)

GND

GND

start/stop
signal

LIGHT SPEED
CIRCUIT

resistor R1
100 kΩ

resistor R2
10 kΩ

capacitor C1
1 µF

GND

V_{cc}

pin 7

pin 6
pin 2

555 timer

pin 8 pin 4

pin 1 pin 5

pin 3

pulses to change
the counter value

pin 13

pin 15

pin 8

4017
decade
counter

pin 14

pin 16

pin 11

pin 9

pin 6

pin 5

pin 1

pin 10

pin 7

pin 4

pin 2

pin 3

resistors
100 Ω

R12

R11

R10

R9

R8

R7

R6

R5

R4

R3

LEDs

L5
red

L4
blue

L3
green

L2
blue

L1
red

GND

LED CONTROL
CIRCUIT

Shopping List

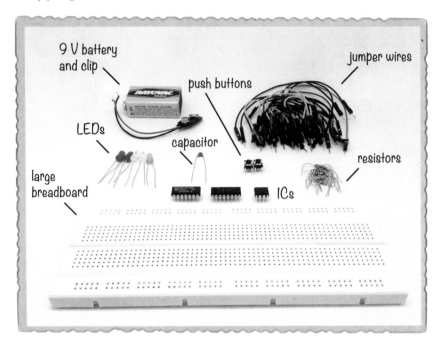

9 V battery and clip

push buttons

jumper wires

LEDs

capacitor

large breadboard

ICs

resistors

- ▶ **A breadboard** (Jameco #2212218, Bitsbox #CN204) with at least 60 rows.

- ▶ **Breadboard jumper wires** (Jameco #2237044, Bitsbox #CN236)—you'll need around 35 for this project. Standard hookup wire works, too.

- ▶ **A standard 9 V battery** to power the circuit.

- ▶ **A 9 V battery clip** (Jameco #11280, Bitsbox #BAT033) to connect the battery.

- ▶ **A 555 timer IC** (Jameco #904085, Bitsbox #QU001) to create the timing.

- ▶ **A 10 kΩ resistor** (Jameco #691104, Bitsbox #CR2510K) to set the game speed.

- ▶ **A 100 kΩ resistor** (Jameco #691340, Bitsbox #CR25100K) to set the game speed.

- ▶ **A 1 µF capacitor** (Jameco #768183, Bitsbox #CC006) to set the game speed.

- ▶ **A 4017 decade counter IC** (Jameco #12749, Bitsbox #QU020) to control the LEDs.

- ▶ **Two standard blue LEDs** (Jameco #2193889, Bitsbox #OP033)

- ▶ **Two standard red LEDs** (Jameco #333973, Bitsbox #OP002)

- ▶ **A standard green LED** (Jameco #34761, Bitsbox #OP003)

- ▶ **Ten 100 Ω resistors** (Jameco #690620, Bitsbox #CR25100R) for limiting the current to the LEDs.

- ▶ **A 4011 NAND-gate IC** (Jameco #12634, Bitsbox #QU018) to create the SR latch for starting and stopping the game.

- ▶ **Two 1 kΩ resistors** (Jameco #690865, Bitsbox #CR251K) to act as pull-up resistors for the start/stop circuit.

- ▶ **Two push buttons** (Jameco #119011, Bitsbox #SW087), one for resetting the game and one for playing.

Tools

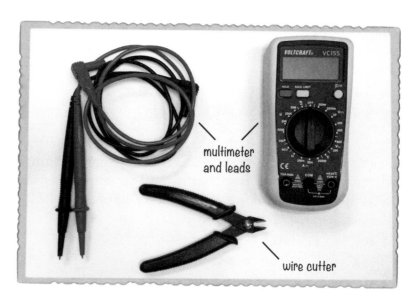

multimeter and leads

wire cutter

- ▶ **A wire cutter** (Jameco #35482, Bitsbox #TL008) to cut small pieces of wire.
- ▶ **A multimeter** (Jameco #2206061, Bitsbox #TL057, Rapid Electronics #55-6662) to debug your circuit if it's not working correctly.

Step 1: Build the 555 Timer Circuit

Plug the 555 timer into the breadboard all the way at the top so that you'll have room for the other parts of the circuits farther down. Then, connect the capacitors and resistors to the IC according to this project's circuit diagram. The capacitor I suggest in this project's Shopping List is a nonpolarized capacitor, so it doesn't matter which way you connect it. If you use a polarized capacitor instead, connect it according to the plus marking in the circuit diagram.

Use wires to make connections as needed, as I show in this breadboard diagram.

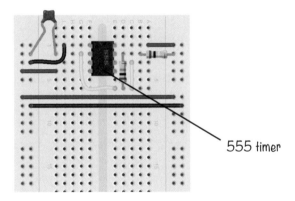

555 timer

In this project, it's best to use the supply column pairs on both sides to make connections easier and keep everything as tidy as possible. The breadboard that I recommend in this project's Shopping List doesn't have blue and red markings, but the positive and negative columns are the same as in breadboards with the stripes. The left and right sides of the breadboard each have a pair of supply columns. The positive supply column is the left column in each pair, and the negative supply column is the right column in each pair. Use a red wire to connect the positive column on one side to the positive column on the other side, and do the same using a black wire with the negative columns.

As you follow my instructions, connect everything in the 555 timer circuit that should connect to V_{CC} to one of the positive supply columns, and connect everything that should connect to GND to one of the negative supply columns.

NOTE *This circuit connects the 555 timer in astable mode, just like the 555 timer circuits in Chapter 8. Read "Meet the 555 Timer" on page 164 for a description of exactly how this IC works. You can also build the projects in Chapter 8 to practice using the 555 timer.*

Before you move on to the next step, check that this circuit is working by connecting an LED with a resistor to the output of the 555 timer as follows:

1. Connect the negative side (short leg) of an LED to the output on pin 3 of the 555 timer.

2. Connect the positive side (long leg) of the LED to a 100 Ω resistor, and connect the other side of this resistor to the positive supply column.

3. Connect your battery clip to one of the supply column pairs as usual. Then plug in the battery to check that the circuit works.

If your LED blinks really fast, then you're ready to move on. If not, recheck your connections to find out where the error is.

When you know the 555 timer circuit works, unplug the LED, 100 Ω resistor, and battery clip.

Step 2: Build the LED-Controlling Circuit

Now, you're going to connect the 4017 decade counter with resistors and LEDs. There are a lot of connections, so take as much time as you need to get them all correct.

Plug the 4017 decade counter into the breadboard so that the middle of the decade counter is around row 20, with the chip marker pointing up toward row 1. Then, take out five LEDs and ten 100 Ω resistors.

Connect each LED's negative (short) leg to the negative supply column on the right, and connect each positive (long) leg to its own empty row in the component area on the right. Place the green LED in the middle, the two blue ones on each side of the green LED, and the red ones on each end.

Then, connect the ten 100 Ω resistors. In the circuit diagram, notice that pins 1 to 7 and pins 9 to 11 of the 4017 decade counter each connect to one side of a resistor. The other side of each resistor needs to be on a row by itself. Take care to ensure the resistor legs don't accidentally touch one another. Look at the following breadboard circuit to see how I connected them:

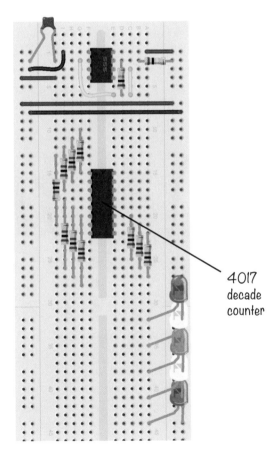

4017 decade counter

Now, connect the LEDs to the resistors on the 4017 decade counter, and connect the decade counter circuit to the 555 timer circuit according to the circuit diagram. Jumper wires are the best way to make those connections.

From each resistor, connect a jumper wire to the corresponding LED. Look at the circuit diagram and notice, for example, that the other side of the resistor connected to pin 4 of the 4017 decade counter should connect to the positive pin of the green LED in the middle. Go through the pins in the circuit diagram to figure out which LED to connect each resistor to.

Connect pins 8 and 15 of the 4017 decade counter to the negative supply column, and connect pin 16 to the positive supply column. Use a wire to connect the output from the 555 timer (pin 3) to the clock input of the 4017 decade counter (pin 14).

Make sure that you have positive and negative connections in all of your power supply columns. The breadboard I recommend in this project's Shopping List (page 267) divides its power supply columns into two sections, one upper and one lower. Just connect each of the upper and lower halves on the left side with a wire to bridge the gap, as shown. Do the same on the right side. Alternatively, use two jumper wires from the left columns to the right columns.

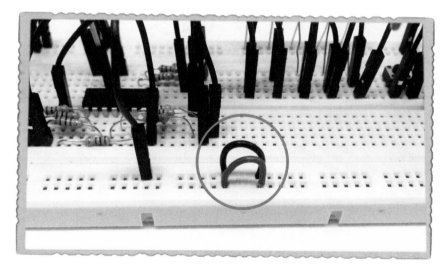

You can use a jumper wire, or you can cut off a small piece of wire, as I've done in this photo. Then, use two long jumper wires to connect the lower-left power supply columns with the two lower-right columns. When you're done connecting the two circuits and all the power supply columns, your breadboard should look like this:

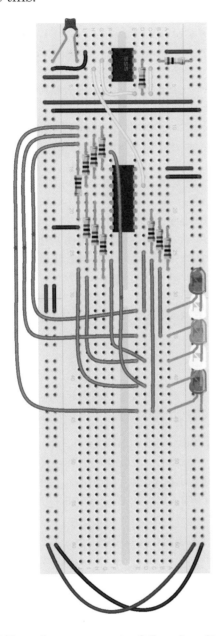

Before building the next part of the circuit, check that your LED-controlling circuit is working correctly, too. To test it, just connect pin 13 on the 4017 decade counter—that is, the "disable" pin—to the negative supply column with a jumper wire, and plug your battery clip and battery into the breadboard as usual. You should see a light "running" back and forth across the row of LEDs.

If no LEDs light up, first check that you've connected the 4017 decade counter with the notch pointing upward. Connecting the chip the wrong way is an easy mistake to make. I've done it many times!

Next, check that pin 16 of the 4017 decade counter is connected to the positive supply column and that pins 8 and 15 connect to the negative supply column. Also, confirm that you've connected the LEDs with their short legs in the negative supply column.

If some LEDs work and some don't, or if the light doesn't run smoothly back and forth, look over all the connections of resistors and jumper wires to find the fault.

After verifying that your circuit works, remove the wire connecting pin 13 of the 4017 decade counter to the negative supply column, and disconnect the battery from the breadboard.

Step 3: Build the Start and Stop Circuit

The last piece of this project is the button circuit that starts and stops the LEDs. Make these connections now:

1. Connect one push button at the bottom of the breadboard, across the notch in the middle. Plug the 4011 NAND-gate IC into the breadboard, a couple of rows above the button. Make sure its chip marking points toward row 1 on the breadboard.

2. Place the second button above the IC on the right component side so that it's easy to reach it with your finger.

3. Connect the two resistors, R13 and R14, as shown in the circuit diagram. Then, use jumper wires to make the remaining connections in the SR latch circuit, as shown in the following breadboard diagram. Connect the positive and negative supply columns to the NAND-gate IC (pins 14 and 7, respectively), and connect the wire from pin 11 of the NAND-gate IC to pin 13 of the 4017 decade counter.

Compare your connections to the following image.

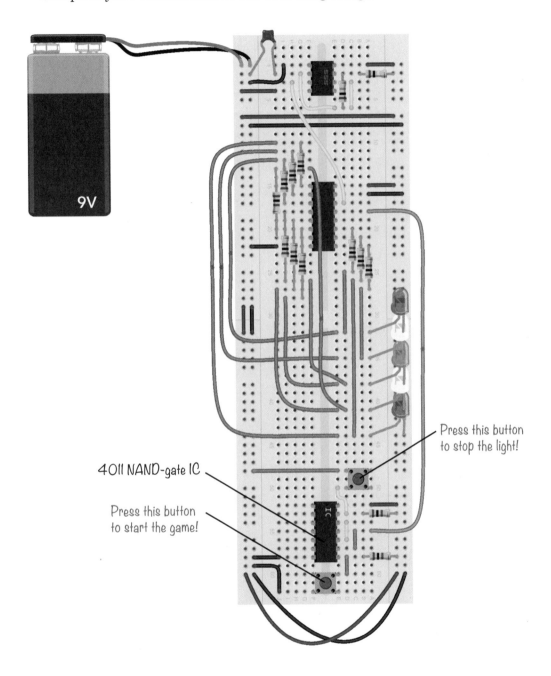

Press this button
to stop the light!

4011 NAND-gate IC

Press this button
to start the game!

Step 4: Practice Your Reaction Time!

All that's left is to connect the battery to the supply columns. The button at the bottom of the board is the Reset button. Use this to start the game and to restart the game after each player attempts to stop the light.

The button next to the LEDs should stop the light when the game is running. See how many turns it takes you to get to 50 points!

Step 5: What If the Game Isn't Working?

If you've followed my instructions so far, the circuits from Steps 1 and 2 should be working. If your circuit isn't working, the only sources of error left are the start/stop circuit you just built and the connection from this circuit to the 4017 decade counter.

A. Check the Continuity

First, check that you don't have a short circuit between the positive and negative columns. To do this, use the *continuity* function on your multimeter. A continuity test checks for a direct connection between two points in a circuit. The symbol for the continuity tester usually looks like the one shown here.

continuity symbol

You don't want a direct connection between the positive and negative columns because that would short-circuit the battery and stop the game from working. Use the continuity tester to check for short circuits.

Turn the dial on your multimeter so that it points toward the continuity symbol. Plug the black measurement lead into the multimeter's COM socket, and plug the red measurement lead into the multimeter's V socket. Touch the tip of the black and red measurement leads to each other, and you should hear a beep to indicate that there's a direct connection.

NOTE *Many electronics enthusiasts also call continuity mode* beep mode.

B. Check for Bad and Good Beeps

Now, plug your battery clip into the breadboard as you would normally, but without the battery. Touch one measurement lead tip to the positive connector and the other to the negative connector. If you hear a beep, there's a short circuit, and you need to fix it! Check all your connections to the positive and negative supply columns.

Next, check the connection between pin 11 on the 4011 NAND-gate IC and pin 13 on the 4017 decade counter to make sure they're connected correctly. Use the continuity tester to check that you have a connection by carefully touching the lead tips on the IC pins. There isn't much space between IC pins, so take care to be sure each tip only touches the correct pin. This time, a beep is a good sign.

C. Check for Power

If the connection to the NAND-gate IC is correct, use a multimeter to measure the output voltage from the start/stop circuit to see whether it's working correctly. Set your multimeter to measure voltage. Make sure the black measurement lead is connected to the multimeter's COM socket, and the red measurement lead is connected to the V socket.

Touch the tip of the black lead of the multimeter to the negative side of the battery, and touch the red lead to pin 11 on the 4011 NAND-gate IC. You should see a high signal—about 9 V—after clicking the stop button and a low signal—about 0 V—after pushing the start button. If not, check the connections of the SR latch circuit to find the error.

TRY IT OUT: CHANGE THE LIGHT'S SPEED

To change the speed and difficulty of the game, play around with different values for R1, R2, and C1 around the 555 timer. Smaller values will make the game go faster. Larger values will make the game go slower. Flip to "How to Set the Output Speed of the 555 Timer" on page 166 for the calculations to figure out specific resistor and capacitor values based on the frequency you want. Note that R1 should not be less than 1 kΩ, as lower values might damage the 555 timer.

But what if you want to change the difficulty on the go? Just replace resistor R2 with a potentiometer. Then you can change that resistance value by rotating the potentiometer shaft, which changes the speed!

ADD A BUZZER TO YOUR GAME

Congratulations: You've finished the last project in the book! Now, it's up to you to decide what to make next. If you're not sure where to start, why not add more circuits to your reaction game?

The LED in the middle is where you want the light to stop, and I suggest adding a sound circuit to bring some excitement to hitting your target. To do this, you could use an active buzzer like the one in "Project #2: Intruder Alarm" on page 11, as shown in this partial circuit diagram.

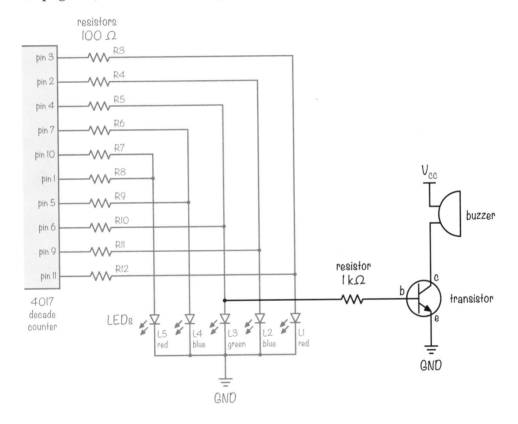

The darker part of this circuit shows new components you'd need in order to add a buzzer to the reaction game project. The lighter components are just a section of the original circuit diagram.

Connect the positive leg of the middle LED through a 1 kΩ resistor to the base of an NPN transistor. Then connect the buzzer to the transistor's collector. Connect the positive side of your battery to the other side of the buzzer, and connect the negative side of the battery to the transistor's emitter.

You should end up with a circuit that makes a little beep every time the light passes the middle LED. If you can stop the light on the middle LED, the buzzer should beep continuously to indicate that you've hit the main target.

When you've customized the game to your liking, solder it onto a prototyping board. Maybe you'll even want to place it in a nice box to hide the electronics and show only the buttons and LEDs.

WHAT'S NEXT? GO MAKE COOL STUFF!

I'm so happy you've read the book all the way to the end! I hope you've enjoyed the projects, and I hope you'll continue building cool things with electronics. One way to practice is to find a circuit diagram for something exciting, buy the components, and build the circuit. You can find circuit diagrams for almost anything online.

I'd also like to invite you to continue learning on my website, *http://www.ohmify.com/.* You can watch video courses, read lots of project tutorials, and visit a discussion forum where you can ask questions and make friends with people from all over the world who also like to build electronics.

Just make sure to ask your parents' permission to join the site, as it's subscription based. If they say yes, then use the following link for a special offer available only to the owners of this book: *http://ohmify.com/e4k/.*

Also be sure to check out the "Online Resources" on page 286—you'll find loads of tutorials and more circuits to build at those websites. Have fun!

HANDY RESOURCES

ere are some resources that you'll find useful when building projects with electronics. Use this as a reference when, for example, you need to figure out what the color bands of a specific resistor mean. I've also listed some websites where you can continue learning and find more projects to build.

COMPONENT AND UNIT VALUE CHEAT SHEETS

Throughout this book, you'll use lots of components, and there are as many ways to read those components as there are component types. Here are some handy cheat sheets to help you read resistors and capacitors and to help you remember what the different prefixes on units like volts and amperes mean.

Resistor Color Codes

Most of the resistors in this book have four color bands. To determine a resistor's value, just look up its colors in the following diagram and multiply accordingly. For example, to get 470 Ω, you'd multiply the number 47 (given by the yellow and purple bands) by 10 (given by the brown band). For more details on resistors, see "Meet the Resistor" on page 70.

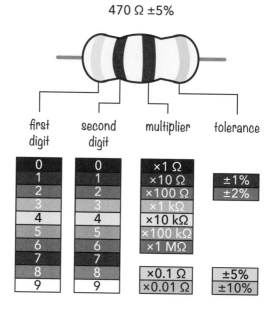

470 Ω ±5%

first digit · second digit · multiplier · tolerance

first digit	second digit	multiplier	tolerance
0	0	×1 Ω	
1	1	×10 Ω	±1%
2	2	×100 Ω	±2%
3	3	×1 kΩ	
4	4	×10 kΩ	
5	5	×100 kΩ	
6	6	×1 MΩ	
7	7		
8	8	×0.1 Ω	±5%
9	9	×0.01 Ω	±10%

Capacitor Codes

In the following table, I've listed the most common capacitor codes. Refer to this table when you're using ceramic or tantalum capacitors because, unlike the electrolytic capacitors used in much of this book, those won't have their capacitance written straight out for you.

Code	Picofarad (pF)	Nanofarad (nF)	Microfarad (µF)
101	100	0.1	0.0001
102	1,000	1	0.001
103	10,000	10	0.01
104	100,000	100	0.1
105	1,000,000	1,000	1

If you have a capacitor with a different code from those listed here, you can find the value in picofarads by taking the first two digits and adding the number of zeros of the third digit.

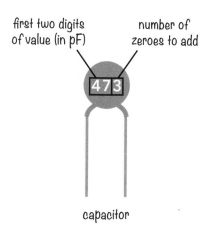

first two digits of value (in pF)   number of zeroes to add

capacitor

In this example, the capacitor has the code 473. Take the first two digits, 47, and add the number of zeros specified by the third digit, 3. That gives you 47,000 pF, which is 47 nF, or 0.047 µF.

Standard Prefixes

When building electronics projects, as in many areas of science, we sometimes have to deal with really small or really big numbers. Fortunately, there's a set of standard prefixes in the International System of Units to make those numbers easier to write. The prefixes are multipliers, as shown in the table.

Prefix	Name	Multiply value by	Example usage
p	pico	× 0.000 000 000 001	Capacitor values (example: 47 pF capacitor)
n	nano	× 0.000 000 001	Capacitor values (example: 100 nF capacitor)
μ	micro	× 0.000 001	Capacitor values (example: 10 μF capacitor)
m	milli	× 0.001	Currents in a circuit (example: 20 mA current)
-	-	× 1	Voltages often don't have a prefix (example: 9 V battery)
k	kilo	× 1,000	Resistor values above 1,000 (example: 10 kΩ resistor)
M	mega	× 1,000,000	File sizes (example: 2MB photo)
G	giga	× 100,0000,000	File sizes (example: 1GB video)
T	tera	× 1,000,000,000,000	Hard disk sizes (example: 2TB hard drive)

A QUICK REVIEW OF OHM'S LAW

Ohm's law is such an essential part of calculating values in circuits that you'll keep coming back to it again and again as you build more projects. Whenever you need a refresher on figuring out a voltage, current, or resistance in a circuit, just flip to this section.

$$V = I \times R$$ Voltage (in volts) equals the current (in amps) multiplied by the resistance (in ohms)

$$I = \frac{V}{R}$$

Current (in amps) equals the voltage (in volts) divided by the resistance (in ohms)

$$R = \frac{V}{I}$$

Resistance (in ohms) equals the voltage (in volts) divided by the current (in amps)

In the Ohm's law equation, you must use volts (V), amps (A), and ohms (Ω), so remember to convert units if necessary: 1 mA = 0.001 A and 1 kΩ = 1,000 Ω.

A BASIC VOLTAGE DIVIDER CIRCUIT

The voltage divider is a circuit that is very useful, for example, when you have a sensor based on resistance, such as a thermistor, which senses temperature, or a photoresistor, which senses light. See "Project #15: Build a Sunrise Wake-Up Alarm" on page 148 for a project that uses a voltage divider like this. You can also use your knowledge of the voltage divider to calculate voltages within a circuit in order to understand what's going on.

When you have two resistors in series, they form a voltage divider. The input voltage gets divided between the two resistors, and the output voltage (across R2) is given by the formula:

$$V_{out} = V_{in} \times \frac{R2}{R1 + R2}$$

ONLINE ELECTRONICS SHOPS

Throughout the book, I recommend shops where you can buy your parts, but those aren't the only great electronics stores in the world! Try these, too:

- Adafruit (US) *www.adafruit.com*
- DigiKey (US) *www.digikey.com*
- Jameco (US) *www.jameco.com*
- SparkFun (US) *www.sparkfun.com*
- Bitsbox (UK) *www.bitsbox.co.uk*
- Quasar Electronics (UK) *www.quasarelectronics.co.uk*
- Rapid Electronics (UK) *www.rapidonline.com*
- Spiratronics (UK) *www.spiratronics.com*
- Farnell (worldwide) *www.farnell.com*
- Protostack (Australia) *www.protostack.com*
- Seeed Studio (China) *www.seeedstudio.com*
- Tayda Electronics (Thailand, US) *www.taydaelectronics.com*

ONLINE RESOURCES

When you're done with this book, you can keep learning about electronics online. (Ask your parents first!) You'll find tons of fun tutorials and other projects at these sites:

Adafruit (*https://learn.adafruit.com/*) Lots of guides based on the components they sell.

Build Electronic Circuits (*http://www.build-electronic-circuits.com/*) My personal blog where I post tutorials, videos, articles, and so on—all about electronics. I also have a free newsletter with useful tips and tricks for your projects.

Electronics Club (*http://www.electronicsclub.info/*) A website for anyone wishing to learn about electronics or build simple projects, created and maintained by John Hewes, the technical reviewer of this book.

Ohmify (*http://www.ohmify.com/*)   My online learning platform with courses, project tutorials, discussion forums, and more. Get cool step-by-step project tutorials, ask questions, make friends, and learn. Owners of this book get a special offer by going to *http://www.ohmify.com/e4k/*.

SparkFun (*https://learn.sparkfun.com/*)   Lots of guides based on the components they sell.

You can also visit this book's website at ***https://www.nostarch.com/electronicsforkids/*** for additional resources, updates, and more.

INDEX

V

V (volts), 6
variable resistance, 144, 145
variable resistors, 146
V_{CC} symbol, 259, 260
V_{DD} symbol, 259, 260
voltage, 5, 6–7, 73
   of batteries, 57–58
   dividers, 146, 147, 285
      calculating the voltage
         from, 147
      measuring light
         with, 148
   how to measure,
      47–48, 54
   from wall adapters, 226
volts (V), 6

W

wall adapter, 226
water, generating electricity
      with, 46
water analogy, for electrical
      current, 9–10
wick, solder, 125
wind, generating electricity
      with, 46
wiper (pin), 145
wire cutter, 26–27
wires
   adding insulation to, 38
   connecting, 16
   hookup, 54
   jumper, 83
   preparing for lemon
      battery, 60
   single-strand, 83
   stripping insulation from,
      26–27

X

XOR gate, 238

Electronics for Kids is set in Century Schoolbook, Filmotype Candy, Housearama Kingpin, TheSansMono Condensed, and Billy the Flying Robot. The book was printed and bound by TC Transcontinental Printing in Beauceville, Québec, Canada. The paper is 70# Husky Offset, which is certified by the Forest Stewardship Council (FSC).

The book uses an Otabind binding, in which the pages are bound together with a cold-set, flexible glue, and the first and last pages of the resulting book block are attached to the cover. The cover is not actually glued to the book's spine, and when open, the book lies flat and the spine doesn't crack.

RESOURCES

Visit *https://www.nostarch.com/electronicsforkids/* for updates, errata, and more information.

MORE SMART BOOKS FOR CURIOUS KIDS!

no starch press

ARDUINO PROJECT HANDBOOK
25 Practical Projects to Get You Started
by MARK GEDDES
JUNE 2016, 272 PP., $24.95
ISBN 978-1-59327-690-4
full color

JUNKYARD JAM BAND
DIY Musical Instruments and Noisemakers
by DAVID ERIK NELSON
OCTOBER 2015, 408 PP., $24.95
ISBN 978-1-59327-611-9

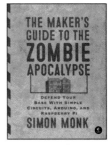

THE MAKER'S GUIDE TO THE ZOMBIE APOCALYPSE
Defend Your Base with Simple Circuits, Arduino, and Raspberry Pi
by SIMON MONK
OCTOBER 2015, 296 PP., $24.95
ISBN 978-1-59327-667-6

THE LEGO® MINDSTORMS® EV3 DISCOVERY BOOK
A Beginner's Guide to Building and Programming Robots
by LAURENS VALK
JUNE 2014, 396 PP., $34.95
ISBN 978-1-59327-532-7
full color

THE LEGO POWER FUNCTIONS IDEA BOOK, VOL. 1
Machines and Mechanisms
by YOSHIHITO ISOGAWA
OCTOBER 2015, 324 PP., $24.95
ISBN 978-1-59327-688-1
full color

PYTHON FOR KIDS
A Playful Introduction to Programming
by JASON R. BRIGGS
DECEMBER 2012, 344 PP., $34.95
ISBN 978-1-59327-407-8
full color

800.420.7240 or 415.863.9900 | sales@nostarch.com | www.nostarch.com